THEORY OF A HAPPY MIND

THE ART OF LIVING HAPPILY

AGRATA SHUKLA

This book is dedicated to all those who have supported me throughout my journey.

To myself, for embracing the challenges and overcoming the obstacles that come with writing. This book is a testament to my perseverance, my love for the written word, and my unwavering belief in the power of storytelling. May this dedication serve as a reminder of the strength and determination that resides within me, fueling my future endeavors. I am almost writing it after an year maybe...but I am glad I did.

Finally, to anyone who has ever dared to dream,

May this book serve as a reminder that dreams do come true with perseverance, passion, and unwavering belief. Chase your dreams, overcome obstacles, and embrace the power of imagination. This book is dedicated to all those who dare to dream big and follow their hearts. May this book be a beacon of hope and discovery, A reminder that within each page lies a world of possibilities, And that through imagination, we find our true selves.

Thank you for being a part of this adventure.

Contents

Contents

About The Author

Agrata Shukla is a multi-talented female author, TEDx Speaker from India, whose literary prowess transcends genres. With her gift for storytelling and profound insights into the human experience, she has established herself as a dynamic voice in the literary world. Her works touch upon themes of self-love, personal growth, mental health, and the triumph of the human spirit. As a psychology graduate, Ms Shanaya possesses a deep understanding of the complexities of the human mind and emotions. Her academic background, combined with her own personal journey, has fueled her passion for mental health advocacy and promoting well-being. Driven by her passion for literature and the written word, Ms Shanaya founded the international monthly magazine "Litvoice." With a vision to provide a platform for emerging writers and diverse voices, the magazine has garnered widespread acclaim, celebrating the power of storytelling and fostering a vibrant literary community.

In addition to her literary achievements, Ms Agrata Shukla is a recognized TEDx speaker, captivating audiences with her powerful talks on mental health, self-acceptance, and personal growth. Her ability to articulate complex emotions and inspire others has made her a sought-after speaker, as she shares her insights and experiences with authenticity and vulnerability. She also expresses her creativity through podcasting, using this medium to engage in meaningful conversations about mental health, literature, and personal development. Her podcast episodes provide a unique blend of insightful interviews, thought-provoking discussions, and practical advice, enriching the lives of her listeners.

Among her notable literary works, "Each Day of Self Love" has resonated deeply with readers worldwide. This transformative guide encourages individuals to embrace self-compassion and develop a positive relationship with themselves, providing practical tools for personal growth and inner healing.

Through her writings, public speaking engagements, magazine, and podcast, she contributes to create a world where mental health is prioritized, creativity is celebrated, and individuals feel empowered to live authentic and fulfilling lives.

Ms Shukla continues to inspire positive change through her writing, speaking engagements, and advocacy work. With a bright future ahead, she aspires to touch the lives of many more individuals, fostering a world where literature, mental health, and personal growth intertwine for the betterment of society.

Foreword

In a world filled with countless challenges, complexities, and opportunities, we often find ourselves searching for guidance, inspiration, and a sense of purpose. It is within this context that I am privileged to introduce this remarkable self-help book—a profound and transformative guide that has the potential to ignite positive change in the lives of its readers.

From the very first page, it becomes evident that the author's voice is not that of an omnipotent guru, but rather that of a compassionate and empathetic friend who has walked the path of self-discovery and growth. Drawing upon personal experiences, insights, and extensive research, the author skillfully navigates the realms of the human psyche and unveils a wealth of wisdom that can be applied to real-life situations.

This book is a treasure trove of practical tools, exercises, and strategies designed to empower individuals to overcome obstacles, break free from self-limiting beliefs, and unlock their full potential. Its pages are filled with transformative concepts, guiding readers towards self-awareness, self-compassion, and a deep understanding of their own unique journey.

What sets this book apart is its ability to bridge the gap between theory and practice. The author effortlessly combines profound psychological principles with relatable anecdotes and actionable steps, making the concepts accessible and applicable to readers from all walks of life. It serves as a gentle companion, offering guidance and encouragement every step of the way.

Throughout these chapters, readers will embark on a transformative journey of self-exploration, learning to cultivate resilience, embrace change, and create a life of purpose and fulfillment. From strategies for managing stress and enhancing relationships to fostering personal growth and embracing authenticity, this book covers a wide range of topics that touch upon the very essence of human existence.

But beyond the practical advice and transformative techniques lies a profound message of hope and possibility. It reminds us that within each of us lies an untapped reservoir of strength, courage, and wisdom waiting to be discovered. It invites us to embark on a journey of self-discovery, to step out of our comfort zones, and to embrace the challenges that lead to growth and personal evolution.

As you embark on this journey, dear reader, I encourage you to approach this book with an open mind, a willingness to explore, and a commitment to your own personal growth. Allow the author's words to resonate within you, and be prepared to unlock the immense potential that lies dormant within. Remember that true transformation requires dedication, practice, and a belief in your own innate ability to create positive change.

It is my sincerest hope that this book becomes a guiding light, illuminating your path towards self-empowerment, happiness, and a life of meaning. May you find solace, inspiration, and the tools you need to navigate the challenges that lie ahead.

With warmest wishes and profound admiration,

Preface

Welcome to a journey of exploration into the fascinating realm of happiness and the mind. In this book, we delve into the theory of the happy mind—a profound understanding of the factors that contribute to our well-being, contentment, and inner joy. Through these pages, I invite you to embark on a transformative quest to unlock the secrets of cultivating lasting happiness in your life.

The pursuit of happiness is an age-old quest that has captivated philosophers, scholars, and individuals from all walks of life throughout history. It is a deeply personal and subjective experience, yet it is also rooted in universal principles that apply to all human beings. It is within the intersection of personal introspection and scientific knowledge that the theory of the happy mind emerges.

Drawing upon research in the fields of positive psychology, neuroscience, mindfulness, and ancient wisdom traditions, this book presents a holistic approach to understanding and nurturing happiness. It is an integration of theory and practice, combining scientific insights with practical tools and exercises that can be applied to everyday life. While happiness is often perceived as an elusive destination or a fleeting emotion, this book proposes a different perspective—one that views happiness as a skill that can be cultivated and nurtured through intentional choices and mindset shifts. It explores the interconnected nature of our thoughts, emotions, behaviors, and the external world, revealing how each aspect influences our overall well-being.

In these pages, we explore key topics such as self-awareness, gratitude, resilience, purpose, and the power of positive relationships. We examine the impact of mindfulness and the art of living in the present moment, as well as the role of values, meaning, and self-compassion in our pursuit of happiness. Each chapter provides practical guidance, reflective exercises, and actionable steps to help you integrate these principles into your daily life.

It is important to note that the theory of the happy mind is not a one-size-fits-all solution. Each person's journey to happiness is unique, shaped by their individual circumstances, beliefs, and aspirations. The insights shared in this book are intended to serve as a guide—a compass to help you navigate your own path towards a more fulfilling and joyful existence. As you immerse yourself in these pages, I encourage you to approach the material with an open mind and a spirit of curiosity. Embrace the concepts presented, reflect upon your own experiences, and allow yourself the freedom to question, explore, and adapt the ideas to suit your own needs and preferences. Remember that happiness is not a final destination but a continuous process of growth and self-discovery. It requires dedication, perseverance, and a willingness to confront and transform the patterns of thinking and behaving that may hinder our well-being.

I am grateful for the opportunity to share this journey with you, and I commend you for taking the first step towards unlocking the secrets of a happy mind. May the insights and tools presented in this book inspire you, empower you, and guide you towards a life filled with genuine happiness, inner peace, and flourishing well-being.

With Love & Grace,

Agrata Shukla

Acknowledgements

Writing a book is a collaborative effort that involves the support and contributions of numerous individuals. I am humbled and deeply grateful for the incredible support and encouragement I have received throughout the journey of creating this self-help book on the theory of the happy mind. I would like to express my heartfelt appreciation to the following individuals:

First and foremost, I extend my sincerest gratitude to my family. Your unwavering love, belief in my abilities, and endless encouragement have been the pillars of strength that have propelled me forward. Your constant support and understanding have enabled me to pursue this project with passion and dedication.

I would like to express my deep appreciation to my mentor, Mr. Avinash Gaurav, Founder of Penvoice. Your guidance, wisdom, and expertise have been invaluable throughout the entire process. Your unwavering belief in the importance of the theory of the happy mind and your guidance in shaping its core concepts have been instrumental in the development of this book.

I am grateful to the team at Notionpress for their professionalism, expertise, and commitment to excellence. Your support in editing, design, and production has transformed this manuscript into a polished and impactful book. Thank you for believing in the significance of the theory of the happy mind and for your dedication to making it accessible to a wider audience.

My deepest appreciation goes to the researchers, psychologists, and experts in positive psychology and mindfulness whose pioneering work has laid the foundation for the theory of the happy mind. Your insights, studies, and dedication to understanding human happiness have provided the framework for the concepts discussed in this book.

I am immensely thankful to the individuals who graciously shared their personal stories and experiences. Your openness, vulnerability, and willingness to share have added depth and authenticity to the book. Your stories serve as a reminder that the theory of the happy mind is not just a theoretical construct but a practical framework that can be applied to real-life situations.

I want to express my gratitude to my friends and colleagues who provided invaluable feedback, support, and encouragement. Your insights, constructive criticism, and belief in this project have shaped its direction and enriched its content. Your presence and friendship have made this journey all the more rewarding.

Finally, I want to extend my deepest appreciation to the readers of this book. Your curiosity, openness, and willingness to embark on a journey of self-discovery and personal growth are the driving force behind the creation of this book. It is my sincerest hope that the theory of the happy mind resonates with you and brings about positive transformation in your lives.

Prologue

"I always wished to be happy in my life, hence I always waited for someone else to give me happiness but with time I understood that happiness comes from within."

Last year I wanted the world to stop, I didn't wanted to enter the New Year and you guys must be wondering about the reason.. well I didn't wanted to grow up, I was desperately looking for a job. I felt this world would fall apart.. I was depressed about it, often cried, in short I was finding happiness.

Today, if you ask me I would say that I consider myself the happiest person alive on the earth. What changed in this one year ?

Well, the answer is mindset. I changed my prospective of happiness.

All humans have a tendency to ruminate more on bad experiences than positive ones.

But that means you have to work a little harder to train your brain to conquer negative thoughts and for that practicing mindset would be the best.

Happiness is a mindset. It comes from within you, not from your outside circumstances. You don't have to have a "perfect" life to be happy. The really great news is that you don't have to be young or old or wealthy or successful in order to be happy. Instead, you can develop a mindset of happiness.

You're going to have roadblocks in your life. You're probably going to fall flat on your face a time or two — trust me, I know what this feels like!

It's OK to fall down. But you have to get back on your journey. And the easiest way to do that is to stay focused and most importantly to love yourself unfiltered. The vision for a thriving life that you love will keep you moving forward, as long as you stay focused.

Your mindset is the combination of your beliefs, thoughts, emotions, assumptions and attitudes. These aren't just your conscious thoughts and beliefs, but also what's in your subconscious.

Your mindset encompasses how you view yourself, your place in the world, the world around you. And that means that it determines your decisions, choices and actions, including how you relate to others and deal with stressful situations.

Your mindset influences (even shapes) your outcomes (which is why mindset is everything).

It's important to understand that having a healthy mindset doesn't guarantee success. Unfortunately, you don't control other people or many of your circumstances. But succeeding in life requires a healthy mindset.

Happiness is YOU. It's attainable for you, even when circumstances are tough. Create your own vision for success this year, make a plan add them to your new year's resolution list, stay focused on your destination and surround yourself with inspiration along the way! It's your time to be happy my love...

CHAPTER ONE

Introduction to Mindfulness

In the fast-paced, technology-driven world we live in, the idea of mindfulness has gained increasing popularity as a powerful tool for managing stress, improving focus, and enhancing overall well-being. But what exactly is mindfulness, and why has it become such a buzzword in recent years?

At its core, mindfulness is the practice of bringing one's attention to the present moment, without judgment or attachment to thoughts or emotions. It is about being fully present in the here and now, aware of our thoughts, feelings, bodily sensations, and the environment around us. In a world filled with distractions and constant stimulation, mindfulness offers a refuge—a way to anchor ourselves in the present and cultivate a deeper sense of awareness and clarity.

The roots of mindfulness can be traced back to ancient Eastern traditions, particularly Buddhism, where it has been a central practice for thousands of years. However, it was not until the late 20th century that mindfulness began to gain recognition in the Western world, thanks in large part to the work of pioneers like Jon Kabat-Zinn, who developed the Mindfulness-Based Stress Reduction (MBSR) program at the University of Massachusetts Medical Center.

Today, mindfulness has evolved into a mainstream practice with applications in various fields, including psychology, medicine, education, and business. Research has shown that regular mindfulness practice can have a wide range of benefits, from reducing stress and anxiety to improving cognitive function and boosting emotional well-being.

One of the key principles of mindfulness is present-moment awareness. This involves paying attention to our thoughts, emotions, and sensations as they arise in the present moment, without getting caught up in past regrets or future worries. By cultivating this awareness, we can develop a greater sense of clarity and insight into our inner workings, allowing us to respond to life's challenges with greater skill and wisdom.

Another essential aspect of mindfulness is non-judgmental acceptance. Rather than labeling our experiences as good or bad, right or wrong, mindfulness encourages us to observe them with an open and compassionate attitude. This attitude of acceptance allows us to be more at peace with ourselves and the world around us, fostering a sense of equanimity and resilience in the face of adversity.

In the following chapters, we will explore the science of mindfulness, the core principles of practice, and practical techniques for integrating mindfulness into our daily lives.

By delving deeper into the theory and practice of mindfulness, we can unlock its transformative potential and cultivate a deeper sense of presence, peace, and purpose in our lives.

Happiness is a universal pursuit, yet it often eludes us in the midst of life's challenges and uncertainties. We find ourselves in a perpetual search for joy, wondering what it takes to attain lasting happiness. The Theory of the Happy Mind offers a profound framework for understanding and cultivating genuine happiness in our lives. This theory goes beyond fleeting moments of pleasure and dives deep into the fundamental elements that contribute to a truly happy mind.

At the core of the Theory of the Happy Mind is the belief that happiness is an inside job. It emphasizes the power of our thoughts, emotions, and perspectives in shaping our subjective well-being. The theory suggests that true happiness stems from cultivating a positive mindset, nurturing emotional well-being, fostering authentic connections, and living in alignment with our values and purpose.

A positive mindset forms the bedrock of the Theory of the Happy Mind. It recognizes that our thoughts and beliefs influence our emotions, actions, and overall well-being. By cultivating positive thoughts and adopting an optimistic outlook, we can shift our perception of the world and find happiness even in challenging circumstances. The theory encourages practices such as gratitude, positive self-talk, and mindfulness to foster a positive mindset and enhance overall happiness.

Emotional well-being is another crucial aspect of the Theory of the Happy Mind. It acknowledges the importance of emotional intelligence, self-awareness, and emotional regulation in achieving lasting happiness. Understanding and managing our emotions allows us to navigate life's ups and downs with resilience and authenticity. The theory promotes practices like self-reflection, emotional self-care, and seeking support when needed to nurture emotional well-being and cultivate a happy mind.

Human connection is a fundamental source of happiness according to the Theory of the Happy Mind. It recognizes the significance of meaningful relationships and authentic connections in our lives. Building and nurturing healthy connections with loved ones, friends, and communities fosters a sense of belonging, support, and happiness. The theory emphasizes active listening, empathy, and vulnerability as essential ingredients for cultivating deep and fulfilling relationships.

The Theory of the Happy Mind emphasizes the importance of living a life aligned with our values and purpose. It suggests that when we engage in activities that resonate with our core values and contribute to something greater than ourselves, we experience a deep sense of fulfillment and happiness. The theory encourages individuals to reflect on their values, set meaningful goals, and make choices that align with their authentic selves to create a life of purpose and lasting happiness.

The Theory of the Happy Mind offers a range of practices and strategies that can be integrated into daily life to cultivate happiness. These include:

Mindfulness and Meditation: The theory advocates for the regular practice of mindfulness and meditation to cultivate present-moment awareness, reduce stress, and enhance overall well-being.

Self-Care: Prioritizing self-care activities such as exercise, healthy eating, quality sleep, and engaging in hobbies promotes physical and mental well-being, contributing to a happy mind.

Gratitude and Positivity: Expressing gratitude and focusing on the positive aspects of life enhances happiness and cultivates a positive mindset.

Acts of Kindness: Engaging in acts of kindness towards others fosters a sense of connection, empathy, and fulfillment, contributing to overall happiness. The Theory of the Happy Mind provides a holistic and practical framework for understanding and cultivating lasting happiness. By emphasizing the importance of a positive mindset, emotional well-being, authentic connections, and living in alignment with values and purpose, this theory guides individuals on a transformative journey towards genuine happiness. It reminds us that happiness is not a destination but a way of being—a conscious choice to embrace joy, resilience, and fulfillment in our lives. By integrating the principles and practices of the Theory of the Happy Mind, we can unlock the doors to true happiness and lead a life of profound meaning and contentment

While happiness is often considered subjective and elusive, numerous theories and perspectives have emerged to shed light on this complex phenomenon. This essay aims to explore the theory of happiness by examining various philosophical, psychological, and scientific perspectives. By understanding the fundamental principles and factors that contribute to happiness, individuals can cultivate a more fulfilling and joyful life.

Hedonic Theory of Happiness:
The hedonic theory of happiness, rooted in ancient philosophical traditions, focuses on pleasure and the

avoidance of pain as the primary drivers of happiness. According to this theory, individuals seek pleasure and try to minimize discomfort or suffering. However, hedonic happiness is often short-lived and reliant on external circumstances. Pursuing pleasure alone may not lead to lasting fulfillment.

Eudaimonic Theory of Happiness:

The eudaimonic theory of happiness, inspired by Aristotle's philosophy, emphasizes the pursuit of a meaningful life and the realization of one's potential as the key to happiness. It suggests that happiness arises from engaging in activities that align with one's values, strengths, and purpose. Eudaimonic happiness is characterized by a sense of fulfillment, personal growth, and contribution to something greater than oneself.

Subjective Well-being Theory:

Subjective well-being (SWB) theory focuses on individuals' self-reported evaluations of their life satisfaction and happiness. It considers happiness as a subjective experience influenced by cognitive judgments and affective states. SWB theory suggests that happiness is determined by a combination of external circumstances (such as income and social relationships) and internal factors (such as personality traits and cognitive processes).

Positive Psychology and Happiness:

Positive psychology, a relatively recent field of study, aims to understand and enhance well-being, including happiness. It focuses on positive emotions, character strengths, and the cultivation of a meaningful life. Positive psychology emphasizes the importance of gratitude, resilience, optimism, mindfulness, and positive relationships in fostering happiness.

Psychological Factors Influencing Happiness:

Various psychological factors contribute to happiness:

Personality traits: Certain traits, such as extraversion, optimism, and self-esteem, are associated with higher levels of happiness.

Psychological resilience: The ability to bounce back from adversity and cope with life's challenges plays a crucial role in happiness.

Mindfulness and flow: Being fully present in the moment (mindfulness) and experiencing a state of optimal engagement (flow) contribute to happiness.

Self-compassion: Treating oneself with kindness, acceptance, and understanding enhances overall well-being and happiness.

Social Factors Influencing Happiness:

Social relationships and interactions significantly impact happiness:

Social connections: Having supportive relationships, strong social networks, and a sense of belonging contribute to happiness.

Altruism and prosocial behavior: Engaging in acts of kindness, compassion, and helping others promotes happiness.

Social comparisons: Constantly comparing oneself to others can lead to dissatisfaction, while focusing on personal growth and progress promotes happiness.

The Role of Culture and Context:

Culture and context influence the perception and pursuit of happiness:

Cultural values: Different cultures prioritize varying aspects of happiness, such as individual achievement, collective harmony, or spiritual fulfillment.

Socioeconomic factors: Income, education, and access to resources can influence happiness levels, but the correlation is complex and subject to adaptation.

Life circumstances: Life events and transitions, such as marriage, parenthood, and retirement, can affect happiness temporarily, but individuals tend to adapt over time.

The Importance of Mindset and Choice:

The theory of happiness recognizes the significance of mindset and intentional choices:

Growth mindset: Embracing a growth mindset, believing in personal development, and seeing challenges as opportunities for learning contribute to happiness.

Autonomy and control: Having a sense of autonomy and control over one's life choices is crucial for happiness.

Gratitude and positive outlook: Cultivating gratitude, focusing on the positive aspects of life, and practicing optimism enhance happiness.

The theory of happiness encompasses a broad range of perspectives, including hedonic and eudaimonic theories, subjective well-being, positive psychology, and cultural influences. While external circumstances and genetics may influence happiness to some extent, internal factors such as mindset, personal choices, and social connections play a vital role in cultivating lasting happiness. By understanding and applying the principles and factors discussed in this essay, individuals can embark on a journey toward greater happiness, fulfillment, and well-being. Remember, happiness is not merely a destination to reach but a continuous process of growth, self-discovery, and embracing life's joys and challenges.

"The theory of mindfulness reminds us: we are not separate from the world around us, but intimately interconnected with all of life."

CHAPTER TWO

Understanding Your Mind

Understanding your mind is akin to exploring a vast, intricate labyrinth, where each turn reveals new corridors of thoughts, emotions, and perceptions. The human mind is a complex amalgamation of neural networks, shaped by genetics, environment, and experience. It's a dynamic entity, constantly adapting and evolving, yet often shrouded in mystery and enigma. Delving into the depths of one's mind is a journey of self-discovery, an odyssey that unfolds layers of consciousness and unconsciousness, illuminating the essence of one's being.

The human mind is one of the most intricate and mysterious elements of our existence. It is not a physical object you can touch or see, but it influences everything we do, think, feel, and imagine. From our daily decisions to our wildest dreams, the mind is the silent force driving our experience of life. Understanding the mind isn't only a scientific endeavor—it's a personal journey. To understand your mind is to begin understanding who you truly are, why you behave the way you do, and how you can make better choices for a healthier, more fulfilling life.

The mind is often confused with the brain, but while the brain is the physical organ housed inside the skull, the mind is a more abstract concept. It includes our thoughts, emotions, memories, beliefs, and awareness. The mind arises from the activity of the brain, but it cannot be reduced entirely to neurons firing or chemical signals. Just like the software on a computer cannot be seen by examining its hardware alone, the mind cannot be fully understood by looking only at the brain's structure. However, studying the brain does give us important clues.

The way the mind interprets time also has a profound impact on how we live. Most of the time, we are caught between thoughts of the past and worries about the future. Regret, guilt, nostalgia, and longing come from mentally living in the past. Anxiety, fear, and anticipation come from imagining the future. While it's important to reflect and plan, spending too much time in either direction pulls us away from the present moment. The only place we can take action and feel alive is now. Learning to anchor your mind in the present brings peace and clarity.

Another crucial part of understanding your mind is the realization that thoughts are not facts. Just because you think something does not make it true. Our minds produce thousands of thoughts each day, many of them repetitive, exaggerated, or inaccurate. A simple thought like "I'm going to fail" can trigger fear and hesitation if we believe it without question. But when we learn to observe thoughts rather than get swept away by them, we can ask: Is this thought helpful? Is it accurate? What evidence do I have? This shift in thinking can reduce suffering and improve decision-making.

Language is another tool the mind uses to organize experience. Words give shape to thoughts. The language we use affects how we interpret reality. Saying "I am anxious" implies identity, while saying "I am feeling anxious" implies a temporary state. Small differences in phrasing can change how we feel. Language can empower or disempower, build bridges or walls. Becoming more conscious of the words you use—especially in your internal dialogue—can change the way you relate to yourself and the world.

Beliefs are another structure that shapes the mind. Beliefs are mental models we create to explain how things work. Some beliefs are empowering, like "I can grow through effort." Others are limiting, like "I'm not smart enough." Many of our beliefs are formed in childhood, based on what we're taught or what we experience. Over time, they become invisible frameworks for how we see ourselves, others, and life itself. Questioning old beliefs and updating them with experience is part of mental maturity. A flexible mind allows room for growth and new perspectives.

Habits are behaviors that have become automatic through repetition, and they are deeply embedded in the mind. The more you do something, the easier it becomes for your brain to repeat it. This is because of a principle known as neuroplasticity—the brain's ability to rewire itself based on experience. Habits can work for or against us. Healthy habits like exercise, reading, or mindfulness can support well-being, while unhealthy habits like procrastination or negative self-talk can sabotage it. Understanding how habits form—and how to replace them—gives you a powerful way to shape your mind.

Emotion regulation is another vital skill in mental development. Emotions are natural responses, but how we handle them determines much of our mental health. Suppressing emotions can lead to inner conflict and physical stress, while acting impulsively on them can damage relationships. Emotion regulation involves recognizing what you feel, understanding why you feel it, and choosing how to express it. Techniques like deep breathing, journaling, talking to a friend, or taking a mindful pause help you respond rather than react. The more you practice emotional awareness, the more resilience you build.

Stress is one of the most common mental challenges in modern life. Our minds interpret stress as a threat—even when the danger isn't physical. The same reaction that once helped humans escape predators is now triggered by deadlines, traffic, or social pressure. Chronic stress floods the body with hormones like cortisol, which can impair memory, concentration, and immune function. Managing stress involves calming the mind. Practices like mindfulness meditation, physical activity, and relaxation techniques signal to the brain that it's safe to relax. A calm mind is a clearer mind.

One of the most transformative realizations in the journey of understanding your mind is the discovery that you are not your thoughts. You are the awareness behind them. This insight, found in many spiritual and psychological traditions, allows you to step back from mental noise and find peace. When you identify with every passing thought or emotion, you are constantly tossed around by your mind. But when you realize you can witness your mental activity without becoming it, you gain freedom. You become the sky, not the storm passing through.

The ego is a central feature of the mind. It's the mental construct of "I" or "me." The ego helps us function in the world, make decisions, and protect ourselves. But when the ego becomes rigid or defensive, it can cause suffering. A fragile ego is easily threatened, constantly comparing itself to others, always needing to prove something. True self-worth doesn't come from the ego but from self-understanding and compassion. By observing the ego instead of being ruled by it, we find inner peace and deeper connections with others.

Another fascinating element of the mind is imagination. Our ability to create mental images of things that don't yet exist sets us apart from other species. Imagination fuels creativity, empathy, innovation, and problem-solving. It also allows us to simulate possibilities before making decisions. When directed positively, imagination builds dreams, relationships, and breakthroughs. But when directed negatively, it feeds fear and anxiety. Learning to guide your imagination—through visualization, creative practice, or hopeful thinking—can improve your mood and motivation.

The subconscious mind is always learning. Even when you're not paying attention, it picks up cues, forms associations, and reinforces patterns. This is how things like driving, typing, or playing a musical instrument become second nature. It's also how fears and phobias form—through repeated exposure or trauma. Reprogramming the subconscious takes time and consistency. Techniques like positive affirmations, hypnotherapy, and behavioral conditioning can help replace harmful patterns with helpful ones.

Dreams are another doorway to the unconscious mind. While the exact function of dreams is still debated, many psychologists believe they help the brain process emotions, memories, and unresolved issues. Some dreams replay the day's events, while others reveal deeper symbolic content.

Paying attention to your dreams can offer insights into what your subconscious is trying to process. Keeping a dream journal, for example, can help identify recurring themes and bring unconscious material into awareness.

Intuition is the mind's ability to understand something without conscious reasoning. It's the sense of "just knowing" something without being sure why. Intuition often arises from experience and pattern recognition. The more familiar you are with a situation, the more likely your intuition will be accurate. However, intuition is not always right, especially when influenced by emotion or bias. Balancing intuition with critical thinking gives you a fuller picture. Trusting your gut is powerful—but it's even more powerful when checked by reflection.

The inner critic is another feature of the mind that can either push us toward growth or trap us in fear. This voice often mimics judgments we've internalized from parents, teachers, or society. While some level of self-evaluation is healthy, constant criticism can lead to self-doubt, anxiety, or depression. The good news is that the inner critic can be transformed into an inner coach. By responding to self-criticism with curiosity instead of shame, we create space for compassion and growth. You can train your mind to speak to yourself the way you'd speak to someone you love.

Spiritual traditions from around the world offer their own interpretations of the mind. In Buddhism, the mind is seen as a flowing stream of consciousness that can be calmed through meditation. In Hindu philosophy, the mind (manas) is part of a larger system that includes intellect, ego, and consciousness. Western psychology, particularly Jungian thought, explores the collective unconscious and the integration of the self. While the language and models differ, a common theme emerges: the mind is both powerful and capable of transformation.

Silence is a powerful teacher of the mind. In silence, the constant stream of thoughts becomes more visible. We begin to hear what's really going on inside. At first, silence can feel uncomfortable. It exposes the restless nature of the thinking mind. But over time, silence reveals clarity. It allows insights to emerge. Practices like meditation, solitude, or quiet walks in nature help cultivate this kind of listening. Understanding your mind means not only feeding it with knowledge, but also giving it space to rest and reveal itself.

Creativity is another way the mind expresses itself. Whether through art, writing, music, or problem-solving, creativity taps into a deeper part of the psyche. It allows us to express emotions that words cannot capture, explore ideas beyond logic, and connect with others across boundaries. Engaging in creative activities activates different areas of the brain and improves mental flexibility. You don't have to be a professional artist to benefit. The act of creating itself is healing. It reconnects you with your inner world and gives voice to what lives in your mind.

Learning is one of the mind's greatest strengths. The ability to absorb new information, adapt, and grow is a lifelong gift. But not all learning is conscious. We learn through experience, observation, and even suffering. Every mistake carries a lesson. Every success builds confidence. A growth mindset—the belief that you can develop your abilities through effort—empowers the mind to keep evolving. Understanding your mind means understanding that you are never finished. There is always more to discover, both about the world and about yourself.

One way to understand the mind is by looking at how it processes information. Every moment of our lives, our senses are taking in data—sights, sounds, smells, touches, and tastes. Our mind interprets this information and forms our experience of reality. This process begins with perception. Perception is not just passive reception; it's an active interpretation. Two people can see the same event and perceive it differently based on their expectations, past experiences, or emotional state. The mind filters and colors everything we experience, often without us realizing it.

Closely linked to perception is attention. Attention acts like a spotlight, focusing our mental resources on what seems most important at the moment. However, attention is limited. We cannot focus on everything at once, and what we pay attention to shapes our reality. If we constantly focus on what's going wrong in our lives, we begin to feel overwhelmed and pessimistic. If we focus on moments of gratitude and learning, we begin to feel more hopeful and resilient. Attention, then, is a powerful mental tool—but it must be used wisely.

Memory is another fundamental function of the mind. Memory is not a perfect recording of the past. Instead, it is a reconstructive process. Each time we remember something, we rebuild it based on bits of information, emotions, and beliefs. Our memories can change over time. We might forget details or even add false ones. Emotional experiences, in particular, leave strong imprints on our memories. That's why painful or joyful events are often easier to recall than neutral ones. Memory influences our sense of identity, our relationships, and how we make sense of the world.

Thinking, or cognition, includes reasoning, problem-solving, planning, and decision-making. Our thoughts are often shaped by beliefs and biases. We like to believe we are rational creatures, but much of our thinking is influenced by unconscious shortcuts. These are known as cognitive biases. For example, confirmation bias leads us to seek information that supports what we already believe, while ignoring or dismissing evidence that contradicts our views. Understanding these mental habits can help us become more objective and make better choices.

Another essential aspect of the mind is emotion. Emotions are complex reactions to internal and external events. They involve thoughts, physical sensations, and behavioral tendencies. For example, fear might come with rapid heartbeat, a desire to escape, and thoughts of danger. Emotions help us navigate life. They signal what matters to us. However, unmanaged emotions can lead to impulsive behavior, conflict, or prolonged distress. Learning to regulate emotions is key to mental well-being. This doesn't mean suppressing them but understanding and expressing them in healthy ways.

The mind also includes the unconscious—mental processes that happen outside of our awareness. We are constantly influenced by things we are not aware of. These include deep-seated beliefs, early childhood experiences, and automatic habits. Sometimes we don't understand why we react a certain way until we look deeper. Psychologists like Freud, Jung, and modern neuroscientists have emphasized the importance of exploring these hidden aspects of the mind. Becoming more aware of our unconscious patterns can lead to profound personal growth.

The relationship between the conscious and unconscious mind is a dynamic one. Our conscious mind includes what we are actively thinking about. It's logical, slow, and deliberate. The unconscious mind, on the other hand, is fast, intuitive, and emotional. Much of our daily behavior is driven by the unconscious—walking, talking, even driving a car becomes automatic with enough practice. This division of labor is efficient, but it can also lead to problems if unconscious patterns are harmful or outdated.

Mental health is a major part of understanding the mind. When our mental processes are disrupted, we may experience anxiety, depression, trauma, or other psychological conditions. These issues are not signs of weakness. They are signs that something in the mind needs care and attention. Just like the body can get sick or injured, so can the mind. Therapy, mindfulness, and self-compassion are powerful tools that can help restore balance. It's also important to reduce stigma around mental health and treat it with the same respect we give to physical health.

One of the most powerful tools for understanding the mind is mindfulness. Mindfulness is the practice of paying attention to the present moment without judgment. It helps us observe our thoughts and emotions rather than getting lost in them. When we are mindful, we can begin to see patterns—how stress triggers anxiety, how thoughts affect feelings, how habits form. Mindfulness builds awareness, and awareness is the first step to change. It teaches us that we are not our thoughts—we are the observer of those thoughts.

Self-awareness is a deeper level of mindfulness. It involves not only noticing what we think and feel but also understanding why. It's about knowing our values, our motivations, our blind spots. Self-awareness allows us to respond to life with intention rather than react out of habit. It helps us take responsibility for our actions and make choices that align with who we want to be. Developing self-awareness takes time and honesty, but it is one of the most rewarding aspects of personal growth.

Another important aspect of the mind is imagination. Imagination allows us to create possibilities, solve problems, and envision the future. It fuels creativity, innovation, and empathy. When we imagine what others are feeling, we build connection. When we imagine better futures, we find motivation. Imagination is not just for artists or dreamers—it is essential for everyone. However, it can also work against us. Imagining worst-case scenarios can fuel anxiety. That's why it's important to guide our imagination toward constructive outcomes.

The mind also contains the inner voice—the stream of thoughts that narrates our lives. This voice can be encouraging or critical, kind or harsh. Often, it reflects what we have absorbed from others—parents, teachers, society. Learning to notice and reshape this inner dialogue is crucial. If our self-talk is filled with doubt and criticism, we are likely to feel discouraged. But if we cultivate a voice of compassion and wisdom, we build inner strength. Positive self-talk is not about pretending everything is perfect, but about being supportive to ourselves in difficult moments.

Relationships play a big role in shaping the mind. From infancy, our brains are wired for connection. The way we are treated by others affects how we see ourselves and how we relate to the world. Secure attachments in early life lead to healthier emotional regulation and stronger self-esteem. On the other hand, neglect or trauma can lead to mistrust, anxiety, or emotional instability. Understanding your mind also means understanding how your relationships have influenced you—and how you can build better ones now.

Understanding your mind also involves recognizing the stories you tell yourself. We all create narratives to make sense of our lives. These stories shape our identity. Some stories empower us—"I am resilient," "I can learn from failure." Others hold us back—"I am not good enough," "I always mess things up." Questioning and rewriting your inner story can be transformative. You are not limited by your past. You have the power to choose a new story—one that honors your truth and supports your growth.

The human mind is one of the most complex and fascinating systems in the known universe. It is the seat of consciousness, the generator of thoughts, the regulator of emotions, and the controller of behavior. Despite advances in neuroscience and psychology, we are only beginning to scratch the surface of what the mind is and how it works. Understanding your mind is not just a scientific endeavor—it is a deeply personal journey. It is a quest to uncover the mechanisms behind your perceptions, beliefs, fears, and desires.

In this comprehensive exploration, we'll dive into the architecture of the mind, its connection to the brain, the role of consciousness and the unconscious, cognitive biases, emotions, mental health, and how mindfulness and self-awareness can transform your life. This essay is designed to guide you through the science, philosophy, and practice of understanding your mind—step by step.

At the core of understanding the mind lies the study of psychology, the science of behavior and mental processes. From ancient philosophical inquiries to modern neuroscientific breakthroughs, humanity has strived to comprehend the intricacies of the mind. Sigmund Freud, with his groundbreaking theories on the unconscious mind and psychoanalysis, revolutionized our understanding of human behavior. His concepts of the id, ego, and superego laid the foundation for modern psychotherapy, unraveling the hidden motives behind our actions and desires.

Yet, the mind transcends the confines of empirical observation; it encompasses the realms of subjective experience and existential contemplation. Consciousness, the subjective awareness of oneself and the surrounding world, remains one of the most profound mysteries of the mind. From the philosophical ponderings of Descartes' "Cogito, ergo sum" to the scientific investigations of consciousness as a emergent property of neural activity, the quest to grasp its essence persists.

Understanding the mind necessitates an exploration of its constituent elements: cognition, emotion, perception, and memory. Cognition encompasses the processes of thought, reasoning, and problem-solving, manifesting in the intricate workings of the human intellect. From simple perceptual tasks to complex decision-making, cognitive psychology elucidates the mechanisms underlying human intelligence. Through cognitive neuroscience, advances in brain imaging techniques unveil the neural substrates of cognitive functions, unraveling the neural circuits that underpin human cognition.

Emotion, the tapestry of feelings that colors our existence, is another fundamental aspect of the mind. From the exhilaration of joy to the depths of despair, emotions shape our perceptions, motivations, and behaviors. The study of emotion spans disciplines, from psychology and neuroscience to anthropology and philosophy, reflecting its multifaceted nature. Theories such as the James-Lange theory and the Cannon-Bard theory offer contrasting perspectives on the relationship between physiological arousal and emotional experience, underscoring the complexity of human emotions.

Perception, the process of organizing and interpreting sensory information, constructs the fabric of our reality. From the intricate dance of photons on retinal receptors to the neural processing of auditory signals, perception bridges the gap between external stimuli and internal representations. Gestalt psychology elucidates the principles governing perceptual organization, revealing how the mind constructs meaningful wholes from fragmented sensory inputs. The study of illusions and hallucinations further illuminates the intricacies of perception, highlighting the role of context and expectation in shaping our perceptual experiences.

Memory, the repository of our past experiences and knowledge, is a cornerstone of human cognition. From the fleeting recollections of episodic memory to the ingrained skills of procedural memory, the mind weaves a tapestry of remembered events and learned behaviors. Cognitive psychologists have delineated the stages of memory processing, from encoding and storage to retrieval and forgetting, elucidating the mechanisms underlying memory formation and recall. Neuroscientific research has unveiled the neural substrates of memory, mapping the circuits that mediate the consolidation and retrieval of mnemonic traces.

Beyond its cognitive and affective dimensions, the mind encompasses the realm of consciousness, the subjective awareness of oneself and the surrounding world. From the dreamlike state of altered consciousness to the focused attention of mindfulness, consciousness assumes myriad forms, each imbued with its own qualities and characteristics. Philosophical inquiries into the nature of consciousness, from Descartes' dualism to Dennett's multiple drafts model, underscore the elusive nature of subjective experience.

Understanding the mind is not merely an intellectual pursuit but a deeply personal journey of self-discovery and introspection. Through practices such as meditation, introspection, and psychotherapy, individuals embark on a quest to fathom the depths of their own minds, confronting hidden fears, desires, and contradictions. The cultivation of mindfulness, the nonjudgmental awareness of present-moment experience, fosters insight into the workings of the mind, enabling individuals to observe their thoughts and emotions with clarity and equanimity.

In the age of artificial intelligence and neurotechnology, the quest to understand the mind assumes newfound significance and urgency. From brain-computer interfaces that decode neural signals to artificial neural networks that mimic the workings of the human brain, technological innovations offer unprecedented insights into the mysteries of the mind. Yet, amidst the allure of technological prowess, we must not lose sight of the essence of the mind—the subjective experience of consciousness and the rich tapestry of thoughts, emotions, and perceptions that define our humanity.

In conclusion, understanding the mind is a multifaceted endeavor that encompasses the realms of psychology, neuroscience, philosophy, and introspection. From the intricate workings of cognition and emotion to the elusive nature of consciousness, the mind reveals itself as a labyrinth of complexity and wonder. Through the lens of scientific inquiry and personal exploration, we unravel the mysteries of our own minds, gaining insight into the essence of our being and the nature of human existence.

Positive emotions are more than just fleeting moments of happiness; they have a profound impact on our overall well-being. Research in the field of positive psychology has shown that cultivating positive emotions can lead to increased resilience, improved physical health, stronger relationships, and higher levels of life satisfaction. In this essay, we will explore the role of positive emotions in promoting well-being and delve into various strategies to cultivate positivity in our lives.

Understanding Positive Emotions:

Positive emotions encompass a wide range of feelings, including joy, gratitude, love, awe, amusement, and contentment. They contribute to our overall emotional well-being and play a significant role in shaping our perceptions, attitudes, and behaviors. Positive emotions have a unique ability to broaden our thinking, build psychological resources, and enhance resilience.

The Benefits of Positive Emotions:

Positive emotions have numerous benefits for our well-being. They improve our psychological and physical health, enhance cognitive abilities, and foster positive relationships. Research has shown that experiencing positive emotions can lead to reduced stress levels, increased immune function, improved cardiovascular health, and greater overall life satisfaction.

Cultivating Gratitude:

Gratitude is a powerful positive emotion that involves acknowledging and appreciating the good things in life. Practicing gratitude can shift our focus from what is lacking to what is present, fostering a sense of abundance and contentment. Keeping a gratitude journal, expressing gratitude to others, and reflecting on the things we are grateful for can help cultivate this positive emotion.

Embracing Joy and Pleasure:

Finding joy and pleasure in life is essential for our well-being. Engaging in activities that bring us joy, such as hobbies, spending time with loved ones, or pursuing our passions, can generate positive emotions and enhance our overall happiness. Embracing moments of pleasure and savoring positive experiences allows us to fully appreciate the present and create lasting memories.

Awe and Wonder:

Experiencing awe and wonder in the face of nature, art, or extraordinary events can evoke profound positive emotions. Awe opens our minds, expands our perspective, and connects us to something greater than ourselves. Seeking out awe-inspiring experiences, such as exploring nature, attending cultural events, or engaging in spiritual practices, can cultivate this positive emotion.

Cultivating Positivity in Daily Life:

Incorporating small but meaningful practices into our daily lives can help cultivate positive emotions consistently. Some strategies include engaging in acts of kindness, practicing mindfulness, expressing gratitude, cultivating optimism, focusing on strengths and accomplishments, and nurturing positive relationships. These practices create a positive feedback loop, allowing us to experience more positive emotions over time.

The Power of Positive Self-Talk:

Our internal dialogue significantly influences our emotions and well-being. Practicing positive self-talk involves replacing negative and self-defeating thoughts with positive and affirming ones. By consciously challenging negative beliefs, reframing challenges as opportunities, and nurturing self-compassion, we can cultivate positive emotions and build a healthier self-image.

Finding Meaning and Purpose:

Having a sense of meaning and purpose in life is crucial for overall well-being. Engaging in activities aligned with our values and passions allows us to experience a sense of fulfillment and purpose. Pursuing meaningful goals, volunteering, or engaging in acts of service can generate positive emotions and contribute to our overall well-being.

Embracing Positive Mindsets:

Developing positive mindsets, such as resilience, optimism, and growth mindset, can foster positive emotions and enhance well-being. Resilience helps us bounce back from adversity, optimism allows us to see opportunities in challenges, and a growth mindset enables us to embrace learning and growth. By cultivating these mindsets, we can navigate life's ups and downs with greater positivity.

Positive emotions are not fleeting moments of happiness; they are powerful contributors to our overall well-being. By understanding the benefits of positive emotions and actively cultivating them in our lives through gratitude, joy, love, awe, and connection, we can experience greater happiness, resilience, and life satisfaction. Embracing positive emotions and integrating strategies like gratitude practice, savoring joyful moments, nurturing positive relationships, seeking awe, and fostering positive mindsets can lead to a more fulfilling and flourishing life. Let positivity be a guiding force in your journey towards well-being and a happier life.

There's a lot to be said for being happy. It makes you better at your job, healthier, likelier to have good relationships, and can even extend your life. Plus, if you've tried both being happy and unhappy, then you already know being happy is much more fun.

Knowing that happiness is good for you won't make you happier, of course. If you're unhappy to begin with, thinking that you're missing out on all the benefits of happiness can just make you feel worse.

There are times in our lives when it's normal to feel sadness, and we shouldn't try to talk ourselves out of it. If you've just lost a loved one, are going through a breakup, have lost your job, or have suffered another adverse life event, feeling sad is healthy and natural. Conversely, if you've been unhappy for a long time and don't know why, or you think you may be battling depression, it's smart to seek out a professional therapist or counselor to help you sort things out.

But for many of us, happiness is a habit that we can cultivate. That's because, thanks to evolution, the human brain is designed to pay more attention to negative thoughts and stimuli than positive ones. It's worth learning how to pay more attention to the positive thoughts in our brains and stimuli in our lives because our natural tendency is to downplay them. That makes us unhappier than we should be.

In a thought-provoking post on the Psychology Today website, Tchiki Davis, PhD, a consultant and expert on happiness technology, offers several simple techniques that will get you thinking positive and increase your general happiness. You can find the full list here. These are some of my favorites:

1. Ask yourself if you're thinking positive.

It's an important issue to consider, and on her website, Davis offers a simple self-assessment that will help you figure out just how much of a positive thinker you are (or aren't). But beyond that, the simple act of asking the question will help you start thinking more positive thoughts more often. That's because of a phenomenon called metacognition, a fancy word for thinking about thinking, which is a powerful memory aid. Asking yourself regularly whether you're thinking positively will help you remember to focus on the positive. That's a great first step.

2. Memorize a list of happy words.

It may sound unlikely that simply memorizing lists of words associated with happiness would be enough to make you happier, and yet it can. Davis explains:

It's because when you force your brain to use positive words frequently, you make these words (and their basic meaning) more accessible, more connected, and more easily activated in your brain. So when you go to retrieve a word or idea from your memory, positive ones can come to the top more easily.

I'm guessing you can come up with plenty of words that you associate with happiness, but if your vocabulary fails you, here's a lengthy list of words that psychologists have measured on the "valence" scale, with higher numbers signaling greater positivity. Not surprisingly, love, joy, and baby are among the highest scorers.

3. Use associations.

Ivan Pavlov famously trained his dogs to drool whenever he rang a bell, by associating the sound of the bell with food in their minds. You can train yourself the same way, creating associations that you can use to your own advantage.

Here's a simple example I used on myself: After a weekend meditation workshop, I wanted to give myself random reminders to be in the moment and enjoy the world around me. So I assigned that function to crows, both because I see them fairly often in the rural/suburban neighborhood where I live, and also because they are very special, extremely intelligent birds. I'm left-brain dominated and analytical, and very bad at simply enjoying the moment. But, even two years later, every time I see crows while driving down the road, I get an instant reminder to live in the moment and enjoy this life while I can.

4. Practice gratitude.

There's plenty of evidence that being grateful for the good things in your life, even very simple things, will make you happier. So every morning before getting out of bed, I mentally list three things I'm thankful for. Some friends of ours ask each family member to say something they're grateful for before eating dinner every evening. There are all kinds of ways to give yourself a daily reminder to focus on something you have to be grateful for. Pick one that works for you.

5. Spend a few minutes each day writing about something that made you happy.

In a fascinating experiment, subjects were asked to spend 20 minutes every day writing about an "intensely positive" experience. A control group was simply asked to write about a neutral topic. The group who wrote about positive experiences reported greater levels of happiness-- and made fewer trips to the doctor over the next three months.

So it's well worth the time to spend a few minutes each day writing about something that made you truly happy. Similarly, Davis suggests savoring as a daily practice--when someone gives you a gift or pays you a compliment, to stop and dwell on how good these things make you feel. Or else, spend some time thinking about a delightful experience from your past.

6. Celebrate your successes, even the small ones.

You can begin with the items on this list. If you've started practicing gratitude on a regular basis (even if it isn't every day) or you've spent some time writing about positive experiences--take that as a win, and an event worth celebrating. Davis says we have a tendency to minimize our own accomplishments (I know I do), and that we should fight that tendency by going out of our way to congratulate ourselves when we do something right.

She also recommends giving up all-or-nothing thinking, which is a great way to make ourselves unhappy unnecessarily. Say you decided to write about a positive experience every day last week. But then you only did it on Monday, Tuesday, Wednesday, and Friday. Our human tendency is to berate ourselves over the three days we missed instead of congratulating ourselves for the four days we met our goal.

So fight that tendency by congratulating and even rewarding yourself for the four days you did do the exercise rather than focusing on the three days you didn't. This is the nature of success. There will be detours and missed opportunities, and I can pretty much guarantee that you will fail to meet your own expectations. It's almost never a straight line from where you are to where you want to be. Making sure you enjoy the small achievements along the way is one of the surest ways to make yourself as happy as you can be.

"Mindfulness is the practice of tending to the garden of our minds, pulling out the weeds of negativity and planting seeds of joy."

CHAPTER THREE

Principles of Mindfulness

Mindfulness is the art of being fully present in the moment, with openness, curiosity, and acceptance. It is both a state of awareness and a practice that helps us return to ourselves, again and again. In a world that constantly pulls us toward distraction, speed, and mental noise, mindfulness offers a return to stillness, clarity, and connection. While the concept of mindfulness has ancient roots, particularly in Buddhist teachings, its principles are universal and increasingly supported by science and psychology. Understanding the principles of mindfulness helps us apply it in daily life—not just during meditation, but in how we speak, work, listen, and live.

The first and most foundational principle of mindfulness is presence. Presence means bringing your full attention to what is happening right now. It is a shift from doing to being. Most of us live with our minds in the past or future, replaying old memories or worrying about what's next. This mental time travel creates stress, regret, and anxiety. Presence invites us to notice what is actually here: the breath entering and leaving the body, the feeling of our feet on the ground, the sound of a bird outside the window.

When we are present, we stop missing our lives as they unfold.

Non-judgment is another core principle of mindfulness. The human mind is naturally evaluative—it likes to label things as good or bad, pleasant or unpleasant, success or failure. While this tendency helps us make decisions, it also creates suffering when we attach too tightly to these judgments. Mindfulness asks us to observe without labeling. Instead of thinking "this is a bad thought" or "this is a good emotion," we simply notice: "this is a thought," "this is an emotion." This gentle observing reduces inner conflict and opens space for wisdom. We become less reactive and more compassionate—toward ourselves and others.

Acceptance is closely related to non-judgment. It doesn't mean passive resignation or giving up. Instead, acceptance in mindfulness means acknowledging things as they are, without trying to push them away or cling to them. When we resist reality, we create tension and suffering. When we accept what is happening—whether it's a difficult emotion, a physical sensation, or an unexpected change—we make room for healing. Acceptance is not about liking everything. It's about being honest with what is here, which paradoxically gives us more power to respond with clarity and courage.

Curiosity is another important principle in mindfulness. Instead of seeing experiences as repetitive or boring, we approach them with beginner's mind—as if seeing them for the first time. When we pay attention with curiosity, even ordinary moments become rich and alive. The breath becomes a source of wonder. A conversation becomes a chance to learn. A difficult moment becomes an opportunity to grow. Curiosity turns mindfulness from a chore into a discovery. It invites us to explore the present moment with openness rather than resistance.

Patience is a quiet strength that supports mindfulness. The mind wants quick results, instant answers, and immediate relief. But mindfulness is not about rushing to fix things. It is about sitting with what is, even when it's uncomfortable. Just as a seed needs time to grow into a tree, the benefits of mindfulness unfold gradually. Patience allows us to trust the process. It helps us stay present with pain, boredom, or restlessness without running away. With patience, we realize that everything changes, and that moments of difficulty often pass on their own.

Trust is another principle that grounds mindfulness. This includes trust in our own inner wisdom—our body, our feelings, and our ability to navigate life. We live in a culture that often teaches us to doubt ourselves, to seek answers outside, and to ignore our instincts. Mindfulness brings us back to inner trust. We begin to notice the signals of our body, the truth in our heart, the quiet knowing that doesn't need words. Trust also means letting go of control and allowing life to unfold as it will. We trust the breath, the process, and ourselves.

Letting go is one of the most liberating principles of mindfulness. Much of our suffering comes from clinging—clinging to thoughts, expectations, possessions, or roles. We hold on out of fear, even when it causes stress. Mindfulness teaches us to notice this clinging and gently release it. We let go of the need to control everything. We let go of resentment. We let go of the story that says we are not enough. Letting go doesn't mean detachment or indifference. It means loosening the grip so we can live with more freedom, kindness, and flow.

Gratitude naturally arises from mindfulness. When we are present, we begin to see what we usually overlook—the beauty of a sunrise, the kindness in a stranger's smile, the miracle of breathing. Mindfulness turns our attention to what is already here, rather than what is missing. From this place of presence, gratitude blooms. Gratitude shifts the mind from scarcity to abundance. It is not dependent on perfect conditions. Even in difficult times, mindfulness helps us find something to be grateful for: a lesson learned, a moment of peace, a breath taken with awareness.

Compassion is both a principle and a fruit of mindfulness. As we become more aware of our own struggles, we also become more aware of the struggles of others. We begin to see that all beings want to be happy and free from suffering. Compassion is not pity—it is the recognition of shared humanity. It leads to kindness in action, gentle words, and a willingness to listen. Mindfulness without compassion can become cold or rigid. But mindfulness infused with compassion becomes warm, forgiving, and deeply human. It connects us not just to ourselves, but to the world around us.

Awareness of the body is a gateway to mindfulness. The body is always in the present moment, even when the mind wanders. By tuning into bodily sensations—the rise and fall of the breath, the contact of the feet with the ground, the tension in the shoulders—we anchor the mind. This embodied awareness brings us out of our heads and into the lived reality of now. The body also stores emotions and memories. Mindful attention to the body can reveal deeper layers of experience and promote healing. When we treat the body as a friend rather than an object, we cultivate respect and care.

Mindful breathing is one of the simplest yet most powerful practices. The breath is always with us. It connects mind and body, thought and feeling, effort and ease. By focusing on the breath, we train the mind to stay steady. When the mind wanders, we gently return to the breath—again and again. This simple act builds concentration, calms the nervous system, and creates space between stimulus and response. In moments of stress or overwhelm, even one mindful breath can shift our state. It is a reminder that peace is always just one breath away.

Equanimity is the principle of balanced awareness. It is the ability to stay centered in the midst of chaos, calm in the face of difficulty, open even in pain. Equanimity is not apathy—it is the strength to feel fully without getting swept away. Life is full of ups and downs. We gain and lose. We love and grieve. Equanimity allows us to hold joy and sorrow with the same gentle hands. It doesn't mean we don't care. It means we care deeply, without collapsing. This inner balance is cultivated through consistent mindfulness practice.

Mindfulness also includes the principle of intention. Before every action, there is an intention. Often, we move through life on autopilot, driven by unconscious desires or fears. But mindfulness asks us to pause and reflect: Why am I doing this? What do I hope to bring into the world? Setting an intention gives our actions clarity and direction. It doesn't guarantee outcomes, but it aligns us with our values. Whether it's the intention to be kind, to stay focused, or to let go of judgment, the act of setting an intention brings purpose to the present moment.

Self-compassion is a powerful application of mindfulness. It means treating yourself with the same kindness you would offer to a friend. Many of us are harsh critics of ourselves, expecting perfection and punishing mistakes. Mindfulness helps us recognize this inner harshness and respond with gentleness. Self-compassion doesn't mean letting ourselves off the hook—it means holding ourselves accountable with care. When we meet our pain with compassion instead of judgment, we create the conditions for real growth and healing.

Integration is the final principle that brings all the others together. Mindfulness is not something we do only on a meditation cushion. It is something we bring into every aspect of life—eating, walking, working, speaking, loving. Integration means mindfulness becomes a way of being. It influences how we show up in relationships, how we handle stress, how we make choices. As we integrate mindfulness into daily life, it stops being a technique and becomes a way of seeing the world. A mindful life is a meaningful life.

Principles of mindfulness encompass a profound understanding of the present moment, rooted in ancient contemplative traditions and modern psychological insights. Mindfulness, derived from Buddhist meditation practices, has gained widespread recognition in contemporary society as a transformative approach to mental well-being and personal growth. At its core, mindfulness involves cultivating awareness, acceptance, and compassion towards one's inner experiences and external surroundings. Through dedicated practice, individuals can develop greater clarity, resilience, and equanimity, fostering a deeper connection with themselves and the world around them.

The principles of mindfulness draw upon a rich tapestry of philosophical and psychological perspectives, synthesizing Eastern wisdom with Western science. The ancient teachings of mindfulness, as expounded in Buddhist scriptures such as the Satipatthana Sutta, emphasize the cultivation of moment-to-moment awareness and nonjudgmental presence. Rooted in the Four Foundations of Mindfulness—body, feelings, mind, and phenomena—these teachings offer a comprehensive framework for introspection and self-transformation.

In contemporary psychology, mindfulness finds resonance in the work of pioneers such as Jon Kabat-Zinn, who developed the Mindfulness-Based Stress Reduction (MBSR) program. Grounded in Buddhist mindfulness practices, MBSR integrates mindfulness meditation, body awareness, and mindful movement to alleviate stress, pain, and psychological suffering. Kabat-Zinn's seminal work has catalyzed a burgeoning field of research exploring the therapeutic benefits of mindfulness across diverse populations and clinical conditions.

The principles of mindfulness are encapsulated in several key tenets:

Present-Moment Awareness: Mindfulness involves directing attention to the present moment with openness and curiosity, free from judgment or attachment. By anchoring awareness in the here and now, individuals cultivate a deeper sense of presence and engagement with their immediate experience.

Nonjudgmental Acceptance: Central to mindfulness is the practice of accepting things as they are, without striving to change or control them. Rather than resisting or suppressing difficult thoughts and emotions, individuals learn to observe them with compassion and equanimity, fostering inner peace and emotional resilience.

Radical Self-Compassion: Mindfulness invites individuals to cultivate a kind and compassionate attitude towards themselves, recognizing their inherent worth and dignity. Through self-compassion practices, individuals nurture a sense of warmth and understanding towards their own suffering, fostering healing and self-acceptance.

Equanimity: Mindfulness fosters a balanced and nonreactive stance towards life's ups and downs, cultivating equanimity in the face of adversity and uncertainty. By cultivating a spacious awareness that embraces both joy and sorrow, individuals develop greater emotional stability and mental clarity.

Intentional Action: Mindfulness encourages intentional and purposeful action, grounded in present-moment awareness and ethical values. By cultivating discernment and wise decision-making, individuals align their actions with their deepest values and aspirations, fostering a sense of meaning and fulfillment in life.

Interconnectedness: Mindfulness fosters an awareness of the interconnectedness of all beings and phenomena, transcending the illusion of separateness. By recognizing our shared humanity and interconnectedness with the web of life, individuals cultivate compassion and altruism, fostering a sense of belonging and solidarity with others.

Continuous Practice: Mindfulness is not merely a technique but a way of life, requiring ongoing practice and commitment. Through regular meditation, mindful movement, and daily mindfulness exercises, individuals cultivate a habit of presence and awareness that permeates every aspect of their lives.

Cultivation of Gratitude: Mindfulness encourages the cultivation of gratitude and appreciation for the blessings and challenges of life. By savoring the simple joys and acknowledging the myriad gifts that abound, individuals cultivate a sense of abundance and contentment, fostering resilience and well-being.

Integration of Mind, Body, and Spirit: Mindfulness invites individuals to integrate mind, body, and spirit into a harmonious whole, transcending dualistic notions of self and other. Through practices such as body scan meditation, mindful movement, and breath awareness, individuals cultivate a holistic awareness that embraces the interconnectedness of mind, body, and spirit.

Commitment to Growth and Transformation: Mindfulness is a journey of self-discovery and personal growth, inviting individuals to embrace change and transformation with courage and openness. By confronting fears, limiting beliefs, and habitual patterns with mindful awareness, individuals catalyze their own evolution and unfoldment, realizing their fullest potential.

These seven principles of mindfulness were introduced by Jon Kabat-Zinn, Ph.D., the creator of Mindfulness-Based Stress Reduction (MBSR). If you're looking for guidance on how to begin working towards these principles, we recommend taking an MBSR class with a qualified instructor who can help you.

1. Non-judgment

It's common to hear we should be non-judgmental of others. After all, you never know someone else's story, what they are going through, or their inner thoughts. But why don't we offer that same grace to ourselves? Have you ever found yourself mad at your own thoughts, maybe saying "a good person wouldn't even think that," or "why can't I just do this/think differently/be normal?" If so, you are not alone, but those judgmental thoughts are not helpful. Mindfulness training can help you look at those thoughts, consider them, and move past them without judging yourself for having them. An important component of mindfulness is that we are not our thoughts. They are simply thoughts.

2. Beginner's Mind

The beginner's mind may be a familiar concept, as it's used in other areas as well. In the context of mindfulness, it is about simplicity. Rather than coming to a situation with the weight of past ideas and experiences, the beginner's mind asks you to arrive knowing that you do not know everything. As no moment is the same as another, every moment allows you a chance to learn. Being open and curious can help save you from being stuck in a rut.

3. Trust

Trust may seem like the odd one out of this list, because so much of these principles is about changing your mindset. Here, we are asking you to trust your instincts. This is actually a natural step with all of the other principles, because in the 21st century, it is all too easy to get lost in the noise of what other people think is "moral" or "right." While adhering to (some) principles and (some) societal norms is an important part of existing in the world, it is also essential that we do not unthinkingly trust principles or norms. The choices you make should be based on your own thoughts and beliefs, not on what the world tells you is the correct way to exist.

4. Non-striving

If you are always reaching for the next thing, never satisfied with where you are, how can you be happy or celebrate a victory? Often, people find themselves trying for another achievement, or another purchase, or "just one more" anything else that will make them finally content, but they never reach that state because of their mindset. Rather than always looking ahead to the next thing, it is important to take time to appreciate the moment. You don't always need to be working to be different or better or anything else. It's okay to take time to enjoy who and where you are. And, once you're no longer always looking towards the future, non-striving can also help you see what is important in the present moment.

5. Patience

The only moment we can live in is the present moment. It isn't possible to predict the future, and ruminating on the past is not helpful because we cannot change what came before. Mindfulness can help you learn to pay attention to the present moment and be truly in it, rather than wishing the future would hurry up and come already or that something will change.

6. Acceptance/Acknowledgement

Acceptance can be a hard one, which is why we've included acknowledgement as another word for the concept. Acceptance does not mean approval or compliance in every situation. As a mindfulness principle, acceptance means seeing the present moment as it truly is, taking it in, and living with that knowledge. You can accept a fact and decide to change it, if that seems like the appropriate choice to you. This principle is not about keeping things the same, but it is about letting go of denial or ignorance and accepting or acknowledging what is happening in the moment.

7. Letting Go/Letting Be

It is way too easy to fixate on things that we cannot change. Human brains are good at that. But ruminating on a situation can become incredibly unhealthy. Rather than fixating, mindfulness can help you accept the present moment and let go of stress. Or, as the alternative suggests, just let the world be how it is

In essence, the principles of mindfulness offer a roadmap for cultivating inner peace, wisdom, and compassion in an increasingly complex and fragmented world. By embodying these principles in daily life, individuals can awaken to the richness and beauty of the present moment, embracing life with greater clarity, resilience, and joy. Mindfulness is not a destination to be reached but a journey to be lived, unfolding with each breath, each step, and each moment of mindful awareness.

"The art of living happily is to savor the present moment, to fully engage with life's experiences, and to appreciate the beauty that surrounds us."

CHAPTER FOUR

The Role of Self-Compassion

Self-compassion is the practice of treating ourselves with the same kindness, care, and understanding that we would offer to a close friend in a moment of difficulty. While many people are naturally compassionate toward others, they often struggle to extend that same warmth and forgiveness to themselves. Instead, they become harsh, critical, and unforgiving, especially when they make mistakes or feel they've fallen short. Self-compassion challenges this pattern. It invites us to turn inward with tenderness rather than judgment and to recognize that being human means being imperfect.

One of the most powerful aspects of self-compassion is that it allows us to respond to our suffering with gentleness rather than resistance. Most people react to personal pain by trying to suppress it, deny it, or distract themselves. This avoidance only deepens the suffering over time. Self-compassion acknowledges that suffering is part of life. Instead of avoiding pain, we learn to face it with courage and care. By holding our pain in awareness and embracing ourselves during difficult times, we begin to heal. Self-compassion becomes a balm for the emotional wounds that life inevitably brings.

Self-compassion is not the same as self-pity. While self-pity tends to magnify our problems and isolate us from others, self-compassion connects us to the universal nature of suffering. Everyone experiences failure, loss, rejection, and hardship. When we remember this, we stop believing that our pain is a personal flaw or punishment. Instead, we begin to see it as part of the shared human condition. This realization helps us feel less alone. It builds bridges rather than walls. We no longer feel like victims of our circumstances but rather participants in the broader human story.

An essential component of self-compassion is self-kindness. This means being gentle and understanding with ourselves when we mess up, rather than being self-critical or harsh. Imagine how you would speak to a friend who is going through a tough time. You wouldn't call them names or tell them they're worthless. Yet many of us use this kind of language toward ourselves. Self-kindness replaces the inner critic with a supportive inner voice. It helps us stay emotionally grounded and gives us the strength to move forward, even after setbacks.

Another key aspect of self-compassion is mindfulness. Mindfulness allows us to observe our thoughts and emotions without exaggeration or denial. When we are mindful, we don't get swept away by our pain, but we also don't ignore it. We allow ourselves to feel fully, without over-identifying with the suffering. This balanced awareness is crucial for self-compassion. It helps us avoid getting stuck in a loop of self-criticism or self-absorption. Instead, we learn to meet each moment with clarity and care, seeing our experiences just as they are—without distortion.

Self-compassion also fosters emotional resilience. Life is unpredictable and sometimes painful. Without self-compassion, we may crumble under pressure or lose faith in ourselves after failure. But when we learn to treat ourselves with kindness and understanding, we build an internal foundation of strength. We become more capable of handling life's challenges because we know that we can rely on our own support. Even when others aren't available or understanding, we have a source of comfort within. This inner refuge helps us bounce back from adversity more quickly and with less emotional damage.

One common misconception is that self-compassion will make us lazy or unmotivated. People often believe that unless they are hard on themselves, they will never improve. But research shows the opposite. Harsh self-criticism often leads to anxiety, depression, and avoidance, which make it harder to succeed. Self-compassion, on the other hand, creates a safe space for growth. When we feel supported rather than attacked, we are more willing to take risks, try new things, and learn from our mistakes. We stop fearing failure because we know it won't destroy our sense of self-worth.

In fact, self-compassion strengthens motivation in a healthy and sustainable way. When we care about ourselves, we want to do well—not to earn approval or avoid shame, but because we value our well-being. This type of motivation is rooted in love, not fear. It fuels progress without the emotional toll of self-judgment. We become our own ally instead of our own enemy. This shift changes the way we relate to goals, setbacks, and success. We begin to pursue excellence with joy instead of pressure.

Self-compassion also improves relationships. When we are kind to ourselves, we become more patient, forgiving, and open with others. It's difficult to give genuine compassion to others when we are running on empty inside. But when we nurture our own emotional needs, we become more available to meet the needs of others. We are less reactive, less defensive, and more capable of empathy. Self-compassion removes the armor we often wear to protect our fragile self-image. In its place, it gives us a softer, stronger heart.

Another benefit of self-compassion is that it reduces perfectionism. Perfectionism is the belief that we must be flawless to be worthy of love or respect. It creates enormous pressure and anxiety. Self-compassion cuts through this illusion by reminding us that we are enough as we are. We don't have to earn our worth by being perfect. Instead, we can embrace our humanity, with all its flaws and contradictions. This doesn't mean we stop striving to grow or improve. It means we do so from a place of acceptance rather than fear.

The role of self-compassion in mental health is profound. Studies have shown that higher levels of self-compassion are associated with lower levels of depression, anxiety, and stress. It acts as a buffer against negative emotions, helping us process them without becoming overwhelmed. Self-compassion also enhances emotional intelligence, allowing us to understand and manage our feelings more effectively. It creates a foundation of emotional safety, which is essential for healing from trauma, coping with grief, and managing chronic mental health conditions.

Developing self-compassion is a practice. It doesn't always come naturally, especially if we grew up in environments where criticism was more common than kindness. But like any skill, it can be learned. It begins with awareness—noticing how we speak to ourselves and how we respond to our own suffering. From there, we can choose different responses. We can ask ourselves, "What would I say to a friend in this situation?" and offer those same words to ourselves. We can place a hand over our heart, take a deep breath, and whisper, "This is hard right now, but I'm here for you."

Meditation and journaling are powerful tools for cultivating self-compassion. In meditation, we practice directing loving-kindness toward ourselves, repeating phrases like "May I be kind to myself," "May I be safe," "May I accept myself as I am." In journaling, we can write letters of support to ourselves or reflect on difficult experiences with a compassionate perspective. These practices help rewire our habitual thoughts and create new emotional patterns. Over time, self-compassion becomes less of an effort and more of a natural response.

The role of self-compassion extends into every area of life. In the workplace, it helps us navigate stress, criticism, and failure with grace. In parenting, it helps us be more patient and present. In creative endeavors, it gives us the courage to take risks and learn from mistakes. In health, it supports sustainable habits and body acceptance. In all these areas, self-compassion acts as a quiet yet powerful force that keeps us grounded, balanced, and connected.

Ultimately, self-compassion transforms our relationship with ourselves. It shifts us from self-judgment to self-understanding, from shame to acceptance, from isolation to connection. It allows us to show up fully in our lives, not because we're perfect, but because we are real. When we are rooted in self-compassion, we no longer fear our flaws or hide our vulnerabilities. Instead, we embrace the fullness of our humanity—with all its light and shadow—and find peace in our own presence.

Self-compassion doesn't mean we never feel pain or doubt again. It means we learn to hold ourselves through those moments with love. It gives us the courage to face our deepest fears and the strength to grow beyond them. It reminds us that we are always worthy—not because of what we achieve, but because of who we are. In a world that often tells us we are not enough, self-compassion speaks a different truth: you are already enough, just as you are.

Self-compassion is a profound and transformative quality that lies at the heart of emotional well-being and personal growth. Defined as the capacity to treat oneself with kindness, understanding, and acceptance in the face of suffering or failure, self-compassion offers a powerful antidote to the harsh self-criticism and judgment that often plague individuals in today's fast-paced and demanding world. Drawing upon Buddhist teachings and modern psychological research, self-compassion has emerged as a key factor in promoting mental health, resilience, and overall life satisfaction.

At its core, self-compassion involves three essential elements:

Self-Kindness: Self-compassion entails being gentle and understanding towards oneself, especially in times of difficulty or distress. Instead of berating oneself for perceived inadequacies or mistakes, individuals with self-compassion offer themselves the same warmth and care they would extend to a dear friend. This involves cultivating a mindset of self-soothing and self-nurturing, embracing oneself with unconditional love and acceptance.

Common Humanity: Self-compassion recognizes that suffering and imperfection are universal aspects of the human experience, shared by all individuals across cultures and generations. Rather than feeling isolated or defective in their struggles, individuals with self-compassion recognize their common humanity, acknowledging that everyone encounters challenges, setbacks, and vulnerabilities in life. This sense of shared humanity fosters empathy, connection, and belonging, alleviating feelings of isolation and shame.

Mindful Awareness: Self-compassion involves holding one's painful thoughts and emotions with mindful awareness, without getting swept away by them or identifying with them. This entails acknowledging difficult feelings with an attitude of nonjudgmental acceptance and curiosity, allowing them to arise and pass away without resistance. By cultivating present-moment awareness, individuals can create a spacious mental environment that embraces both joy and sorrow, fostering inner peace and emotional resilience.

The role of self-compassion extends far beyond mere self-indulgence or self-esteem boosting; it encompasses a profound shift in one's relationship with oneself and the world. Research conducted by Dr. Kristin Neff and her colleagues has demonstrated the myriad benefits of self-compassion across diverse domains of life, including mental health, emotional well-being, relationships, and performance.

In terms of mental health, self-compassion has been linked to reduced levels of anxiety, depression, and stress, as well as greater psychological flexibility and emotional regulation. By offering oneself kindness and understanding in times of distress, individuals with self-compassion are better equipped to navigate life's challenges with resilience and equanimity. Moreover, self-compassion buffers against the detrimental effects of self-criticism and perfectionism, promoting a healthier and more balanced sense of self-worth.

In the realm of emotional well-being, self-compassion fosters greater emotional resilience and flexibility, enabling individuals to bounce back from setbacks and disappointments with grace and fortitude. Rather than ruminating on past failures or catastrophizing about future outcomes, individuals with self-compassion are able to hold their experiences with a sense of perspective and wisdom, recognizing that temporary setbacks do not define their inherent worth or potential.

Self-compassion also plays a crucial role in nurturing healthy and fulfilling relationships. By cultivating kindness and empathy towards oneself, individuals with self-compassion are better able to extend these qualities to others, fostering deeper connections and intimacy. Moreover, self-compassion mitigates feelings of resentment, envy, and comparison in relationships, allowing individuals to celebrate the successes and joys of others without diminishing their own sense of self-worth.

The idea that people need high self-esteem in order to be psychologically healthy is almost a truism in Western developmental psychology. Parents are told that one of their most important tasks is to nurture their children's self-esteem. Teachers are encouraged to give all their students gold stars so that each can feel proud and special. Psychologists worry about the dangerous drop in self-esteem experienced by adolescents as they transition out of childhood and try to find ways to give teens a self-esteem boost. The assumption that high self-esteem is synonymous with well- being applies throughout the lifespan. The elderly benefit from high self-esteem as much as anyone, don't they? The issue is not so simple. In the field of social psychology, scholars are starting to fall out of love with self-esteem. Yes, it is true that high self-esteem is associated with less depression and anxiety, as well as with greater happiness and life satisfaction. However, there are also some dark sides to high self-esteem.

For instance, high self-esteem is strongly correlated with narcissism. Twenge [2006] argued that the emphasis placed on self-esteem in American schools and culture at large is responsible for the creation of 'generation me', so named because of the steady and consistent rise in narcissism levels among American college students documented since the mid 1960s. Self-esteem is also associated with the better-than- average effect, the need to feel superior to others just to feel okay about oneself. Research shows that most people think they are funnier, more logical, more popular, better looking, nicer, more trustworthy, wiser and more intelligent than others [Alicke & Govorun, 2005]. To be average is unacceptable in Western society, so pretty much everyone walks around wearing rose-colored glasses (at least when they are looking in the mirror). This comparative dynamic, however, the tendency to puff ourselves up and put others down, creates interpersonal distance and separation that undermines connectedness.

Recent reviews of the research literature, moreover, have suggested that high self-esteem is not all it is cracked up to be [e.g., Baumeister, Campbell, Krueger, & Vohs, 2003]. Self-esteem does not appear to improve academic or job performance, to improve leadership skills or to prevent children from smoking, drinking, taking drugs and engaging in early sex. Bullies are as likely to have high self-esteem as others, and in fact, hassling other people and putting them down is one way that bullies feel good about themselves. People with high self-esteem are just as prejudiced if not more so than those who dislike themselves. They are also just as aggressive and engage in antisocial behavior like cheating, as often as people with low self-esteem do. Still, we know that low self-esteem can be problematic and in extreme cases leads to suicidal ideation. So what is the alternative?

There is another way of positively relating to oneself that does not involve self- evaluations or social comparisons but, rather, involves compassion. While the concept of self-compassion has existed in Eastern philosophical thought for centuries, it is relatively new in the West. The past decade has seen an increasing interchange of ideas between Buddhism and Western psychology, especially in terms of how mindfulness relates to mental health [e.g., Brown, Ryan, & Creswell, 2007]. Research on self-compassion that my colleagues and I have conducted over the past several years [e.g., Gilbert, 2009; Leary, Tate, Adams, Allen, & Hancock, 2007; Neff, 2009] is part of this exchange. In general, the research suggests that self-compassion offers most of the benefits of high self-esteem, with fewer downsides.

Drawing on the writings of Buddhist scholars, I have defined self-compassion as having 3 main components: (a) self-kindness versus self-judgment, (b) a sense of common humanity versus isolation, and (c) mindfulness versus overidentification [Neff, 2003]. These components combine and mutually interact to create a self-compassionate frame of mind. Self-kindness refers to the tendency to be caring and understanding with oneself rather than being harshly critical or judgmental. Instead of taking a cold 'stiff-upper-lip' approach in times of suffering, self-kindness offers soothing and comfort to the self.

Common humanity involves recognizing that all humans are imperfect, fail and make mistakes. It connects one's own flawed condition to the shared human condition so that greater perspective is taken towards personal shortcomings and difficulties. Mindfulness, the third component of self-compassion, involves being aware of one's present moment experience in a clear and balanced manner so that one neither ignores nor ruminates on disliked aspects of oneself or one's life. Compassion can be extended towards the self when suffering occurs through no fault of one's own – when the external circumstances of life are simply painful or difficult to bear. Self-compassion is equally relevant, however, when suffering stems from one's own foolish actions, failures or personal inadequacies.

Much of the research conducted on self-compassion has used the Self-Compassion Scale [Neff, 2003], which measures self-compassion as a stable trait, although researchers are also starting to use mood inductions to examine self-compassionate states [e.g., Leary et al., 2007]. Research indicates that self-compassion is strongly associated with psychological well-being [Neff, 2009]. Higher levels of self-compassion are linked to increased feelings of happiness, optimism, curiosity and connectedness, as well as decreased anxiety, depression, rumination and fear of failure. While lay people often express the worry that if they are too self-compassionate, they will undermine their motivation or become self-indulgent, this does not appear to be the case. Self-compassion involves the desire for the self's health and well-being, and is associated with greater personal initiative to make needed changes in one's life. Because self-compassionate individuals do not berate themselves when they fail, they are more able to admit mistakes, modify unproductive behaviors and take on new challenges. In a study of self-compassion in classroom settings, for instance, we found that self-compassion was positively associated with mastery goals for learning and negatively associated with performance goals [Neff, Hseih, & Dejitthirat, 2005]. Thus, self-compassionate individuals are motivated to learn and grow, but for intrinsic reasons – not because they want to garner social approval.

Moreover, self-compassion appears to produce psychological benefits without generating the negative effects associated with enhanced self-esteem. For example, Neff and Vonk [2009] found that when compared to trait levels of self-esteem, self-compassion was associated with more noncontingent and stable feelings of self- worth over time, while also offering stronger protection against social comparison, public self-consciousness, self-rumination, anger and closed-mindedness. Furthermore, in direct contrast to self-esteem, self-compassion was found to have no association with narcissism.

While most of the research on self-compassion has been published in social psychology journals, there are reasons to believe that self-compassion could be a useful construct for developmental psychologists. For instance, parenting behaviors appear to contribute to the development of self-compassion. A recent study [Neff & McGehee, in press] found that maternal support, harmonious family functioning and secure attachment all predicted higher levels of self-compassion among teens. Similarly, developmental factors such as adolescent egocentrism – specifically the personal fable – negatively predicted self-compassion. The study also showed that self-compassion partially mediated the link between family factors, adolescent egocentrism and well-being (measured in terms of depression, anxiety and connectedness). This suggests that one way family and cognitive-developmental factors influence adolescent functioning is by fostering self-compassionate versus self-critical inner dialogues.

Self-compassion may also be an important aspect of maturity. Research has shown that self-compassion has a small but significant association with age [Neff & Vonk, 2009]. Perhaps more importantly, self-compassion is strongly associated with emotional intelligence and wisdom [Neff, 2009]. In Toward a Psychology of Being, Maslow [1968] argued that emotional maturity entails fostering nonjudgmental, forgiving, loving acceptance of oneself as well as others. Self-compassion epitomizes this way of being, and may help developmental psychologists understand and foster healthy forms of self-relating throughout the lifespan.

In terms of performance and achievement, self-compassion has been shown to enhance motivation, perseverance, and creativity. Rather than being driven by fear of failure or harsh self-criticism, individuals with self-compassion approach challenges with a growth mindset and a sense of curiosity, viewing mistakes and setbacks as opportunities for learning and growth. This adaptive mindset fosters greater innovation, resilience, and adaptability in the face of uncertainty and change.

Furthermore, self-compassion promotes overall life satisfaction and well-being by fostering a sense of inner peace, contentment, and fulfillment. By embracing oneself with kindness and acceptance, individuals with self-compassion cultivate a deep sense of self-love and authenticity, aligning their actions with their deepest values and aspirations. This sense of inner harmony radiates outward, enriching all aspects of life—from work and relationships to leisure and creative expression.

Despite its myriad benefits, cultivating self-compassion is not always easy, especially in a culture that valorizes achievement, success, and self-reliance. Many individuals struggle with feelings of unworthiness, shame, and self-doubt, which can undermine their ability to practice self-compassion. Moreover, societal norms and expectations often perpetuate myths of self-sufficiency and stoicism, discouraging individuals from seeking support or acknowledging their vulnerabilities.

However, the journey of self-compassion is one of courage, humility, and resilience—a journey that begins with a single act of kindness towards oneself. By practicing self-compassion in daily life—through meditation, self-reflection, and self-care—individuals can gradually rewire their brains and hearts to embrace themselves with greater love, acceptance, and understanding. Moreover, by cultivating self-compassion, individuals contribute to a culture of kindness, empathy, and connection, fostering a more compassionate and inclusive world for all.

In our fast-paced and often self-critical world, self-compassion has emerged as a vital component of emotional well-being and personal growth. Defined as extending kindness and understanding towards oneself in times of struggle or failure, self-compassion offers a powerful alternative to self-judgment and harsh self-criticism. In this essay, we will explore the role of self-compassion in nurturing well-being, enhancing emotional resilience, and fostering positive self-growth.

Understanding Self-Compassion:

Self-compassion involves treating ourselves with the same kindness, care, and understanding that we would extend to a close friend or loved one. It is grounded in three interconnected elements: self-kindness, common humanity, and mindfulness. Self-kindness encourages self-nurturing and self-support, common humanity highlights our shared human experiences and imperfections, and mindfulness cultivates non-judgmental awareness of our thoughts and emotions.

The Benefits of Self-Compassion:

Self-compassion has been extensively researched and linked to numerous benefits for emotional well-being. It has shown to reduce anxiety, depression, and stress, while increasing life satisfaction, resilience, and overall psychological well-being. By offering ourselves warmth and understanding, self-compassion creates a foundation for growth, healing, and positive self-regard.

Overcoming the Inner Critic:

The inner critic is that harsh, self-critical voice that often sabotages our self-esteem and happiness. Self-compassion acts as an antidote to the inner critic by promoting self-acceptance and self-soothing. By cultivating self-compassion, we can challenge the destructive patterns of self-judgment and develop a kinder and more supportive inner dialogue.

Self-Compassion and Emotional Resilience:

Emotional resilience refers to our ability to bounce back from adversity and navigate life's challenges with strength and grace. Self-compassion plays a crucial role in developing emotional resilience by offering a buffer against stress, fostering emotional regulation, and promoting self-care. It allows us to acknowledge our pain and difficulties while providing the support and encouragement needed to move forward.

Cultivating Self-Compassion in Practice:

Cultivating self-compassion is an ongoing process that involves intentional practice and self-reflection. Various techniques can help nurture self-compassion, including self-compassion exercises, guided meditations, journaling, and self-reflective practices. These practices encourage self-kindness, self-acceptance, and the recognition of our common humanity, ultimately fostering a compassionate relationship with ourselves.

Self-Compassion in Relationships:

Self-compassion not only benefits our relationship with ourselves but also has a positive impact on our relationships with others. When we treat ourselves with kindness and understanding, we become more compassionate and empathetic towards others. Self-compassion allows us to approach conflicts and interactions with greater patience, understanding, and forgiveness, promoting healthier and more satisfying relationships.

Self-Compassion in Personal Growth:

Self-compassion is closely tied to personal growth and self-improvement. Unlike self-criticism, which often hinders progress, self-compassion provides a nurturing environment for learning, growth, and change. By embracing our imperfections, accepting setbacks as opportunities for growth, and offering ourselves kindness and encouragement, we can embark on a journey of self-discovery and positive transformation.

The Role of Mindfulness in Self-Compassion:

Mindfulness, the practice of non-judgmental awareness of the present moment, is an integral component of self-compassion. It allows us to observe our thoughts and emotions with curiosity and without judgment. Mindfulness helps us recognize when we are being self-critical and encourages us to respond with self-compassion, fostering a sense of acceptance and inner peace.

Self-Compassion and Self-Care:

Self-compassion is intimately intertwined with self-care. It reminds us to prioritize our well-being, attend to our physical and emotional needs, and set boundaries to protect our mental health. Self-compassion encourages us to engage in activities that nourish and recharge us, emphasizing the importance of self-care as a means to cultivate overall well-being.

Overcoming Barriers to Self-Compassion:

Although self-compassion is beneficial, many individuals struggle to cultivate it due to various barriers. These barriers may include perfectionism, fear of self-indulgence, or cultural and societal expectations. Recognizing these barriers and developing strategies to overcome them can pave the way for embracing self-compassion and reaping its rewards.

Self-compassion is a powerful tool for nurturing well-being, fostering emotional resilience, and promoting personal growth. By extending kindness, understanding, and acceptance towards ourselves, we create an inner environment of compassion and support. Through self-compassion practices, mindfulness, and self-care, we can cultivate a deep sense of self-love and transform our relationship with ourselves and others. Embracing self-compassion is not only a path to personal well-being but also a gateway to a more compassionate and connected world.

"Mindfulness is the practice of deep listening—to the whispers of the body, the stirrings of the heart, and the echoes of the cosmos."

CHAPTER FIVE

Mindfulness and Happiness

Mindfulness is a practice and a state of being that involves bringing one's attention to the present moment, intentionally and non-judgmentally. It is the art of fully engaging with and experiencing the present, cultivating a deep awareness of one's thoughts, emotions, bodily sensations, and the surrounding environment.

Rooted in ancient Buddhist traditions, mindfulness has gained significant attention in contemporary society due to its profound benefits for mental, emotional, and physical well-being. It offers a powerful antidote to the fast-paced, distracted, and stress-filled lives many people lead, allowing them to find peace, clarity, and a sense of connection amidst the chaos of everyday life.

At its core, mindfulness encourages individuals to embrace the present moment without judgment or resistance. It invites one to observe thoughts and emotions as they arise, acknowledging them with kindness and curiosity rather than getting caught up in them. Through mindfulness, individuals learn to cultivate a non-reactive and accepting stance towards their experiences, which can lead to a greater sense of inner calm, resilience, and overall well-being.

Mindfulness can be practiced in various ways, such as through formal meditation, informal daily activities, or specialized techniques like mindful eating, walking, or breathing. The key is to bring a heightened sense of awareness and attention to whatever is happening in the present moment, whether it be the sensations of breathing, the taste of food, or the sounds in the environment.

Scientific research has shown that practicing mindfulness can have numerous positive effects on both mental and physical health. Regular mindfulness practice has been linked to reduced stress, anxiety, and depression, improved focus and attention, enhanced emotional regulation, increased self-compassion, and improved relationships.

It's a busy world. You fold the laundry while keeping one eye on the kids and another on the television. You plan your day while listening to the radio and commuting to work, and then plan your weekend. But in the rush to accomplish necessary tasks, you may find yourself losing your connection with the present moment—missing out on what you're doing and how you're feeling. Did you notice whether you felt well-rested this morning or that forsythia is in bloom along your route to work?

Mindfulness is the practice of purposely focusing your attention on the present moment—and accepting it without judgment. Mindfulness is now being examined scientifically and has been found to be a key element in stress reduction and overall happiness.

Speak to a Licensed Therapist

BetterHelp is an online therapy service that matches you to licensed, accredited therapists who can help with depression, anxiety, relationships, and more. Take the assessment and get matched with a therapist in as little as 48 hours.

What are the benefits of mindfulness?

The cultivation of mindfulness has roots in Buddhism, but most religions include some type of prayer or meditation technique that helps shift your thoughts away from your usual preoccupations toward an appreciation of the moment and a larger perspective on life.

Professor emeritus Jon Kabat-Zinn, founder and former director of the Stress Reduction Clinic at the University of Massachusetts Medical Center, helped to bring the practice of mindfulness meditation into mainstream medicine and demonstrated that practicing mindfulness can bring improvements in both physical and psychological symptoms as well as positive changes in health, attitudes, and behaviors.

Mindfulness improves well-being. Increasing your capacity for mindfulness supports many attitudes that contribute to a satisfied life. Being mindful makes it easier to savor the pleasures in life as they occur, helps you become fully engaged in activities, and creates a greater capacity to deal with adverse events. By focusing on the here and now, many people who practice mindfulness find that they are less likely to get caught up in worries about the future or regrets over the past, are less preoccupied with concerns about success and self-esteem, and are better able to form deep connections with others.

Mindfulness improves physical health. If greater well-being isn't enough of an incentive, scientists have discovered that mindfulness techniques help improve physical health in a number of ways. Mindfulness can: help relieve stress, treat heart disease, lower blood pressure, reduce chronic pain, , improve sleep, and alleviate gastrointestinal difficulties.

Mindfulness improves mental health. In recent years, psychotherapists (both in-person and online) have turned to mindfulness meditation as an important element in the treatment of a number of problems, including: depression, substance abuse, eating disorders, couples' conflicts, anxiety disorders, and obsessive-compulsive disorder.

How does mindfulness work?

Some experts believe that mindfulness works, in part, by helping people to accept their experiences—including painful emotions—rather than react to them with aversion and avoidance.

It's become increasingly common for mindfulness meditation to be combined with psychotherapy, especially cognitive behavioral therapy. This development makes good sense, since both meditation and cognitive behavioral therapy share the common goal of helping people gain perspective on irrational, maladaptive, and self-defeating thoughts.

Mindfulness techniques

There is more than one way to practice mindfulness, but the goal of any mindfulness technique is to achieve a state of alert, focused relaxation by deliberately paying attention to thoughts and sensations without judgment. This allows the mind to refocus on the present moment. All mindfulness techniques are a form of meditation.

Basic mindfulness meditation – Sit quietly and focus on your natural breathing or on a word or "mantra" that you repeat silently. Allow thoughts to come and go without judgment and return to your focus on breath or mantra.

Body sensations – Notice subtle body sensations such as an itch or tingling without judgment and let them pass. Notice each part of your body in succession from head to toe.

Sensory – Notice sights, sounds, smells, tastes, and touches. Name them "sight," "sound," "smell," "taste," or "touch" without judgment and let them go.

Emotions – Allow emotions to be present without judgment. Practice a steady and relaxed naming of emotions: "joy," "anger," "frustration." Accept the presence of the emotions without judgment and let them go.

Urge surfing – Cope with cravings (for addictive substances or behaviors) and allow them to pass. Notice how your body feels as the craving enters. Replace the wish for the craving to go away with the certain knowledge that it will subside.

Mindfulness meditation and other practices

Mindfulness can be cultivated through mindfulness meditation, a systematic method of focusing your attention. You can learn to meditate on your own, following instructions in books or on tape. However, you may benefit from the support of an instructor or group to answer questions and help you stay motivated. Look for someone using meditation in a way compatible with your beliefs and goals.

If you have a medical condition, you may prefer a medically oriented program that incorporates meditation. Ask your physician or hospital about local groups. Insurance companies increasingly cover the cost of meditation instruction.

Getting started on your own

Some types of meditation primarily involve concentration—repeating a phrase or focusing on the sensation of breathing, allowing the parade of thoughts that inevitably arise to come and go. Concentration meditation techniques, as well as other activities such as tai chi or yoga, can induce the well-known relaxation response, which is very valuable in reducing the body's response to stress.

Mindfulness meditation builds upon concentration practices. Here's how it works:

Go with the flow. In mindfulness meditation, once you establish concentration, you observe the flow of inner thoughts, emotions, and bodily sensations without judging them as good or bad.

Pay attention. You also notice external sensations such as sounds, sights, and touch that make up your moment-to-moment experience. The challenge is not to latch onto a particular idea, emotion, or sensation, or to get caught in thinking about the past or the future. Instead, you watch what comes and goes in your mind and discover which mental habits produce a feeling of well-being or suffering.

Stay with it. At times, this process may not seem relaxing at all, but over time it provides a key to greater happiness and self-awareness as you become comfortable with a wider and wider range of your experiences.

Practice acceptance

Above all, mindfulness practice involves accepting whatever arises in your awareness at each moment. It involves being kind and forgiving toward yourself.

Some tips to keep in mind:

Gently redirect. If your mind wanders into planning, daydreaming, or criticism, notice where it has gone and gently redirect it to sensations in the present.

Try and try again. If you miss your intended meditation session, simply start again.

By practicing accepting your experience during meditation, it becomes easier to accept whatever comes your way during the rest of your day.

Cultivate mindfulness informally

In addition to formal meditation, you can also cultivate mindfulness informally by focusing your attention on your moment-to-moment sensations during everyday activities. This is done by single-tasking—doing one thing at a time and giving it your full attention. As you floss your teeth, pet the dog, or eat an apple, slow down the process and be fully present as it unfolds and involves all of your senses.

Mindfulness exercises

If mindfulness meditation appeals to you, going to a class or listening to a meditation tape can be a good way to start. In the meantime, here are two mindfulness exercises you can try on your own.

Basic mindfulness meditation

This exercise teaches basic mindfulness meditation.

Sit on a straight-backed chair or cross-legged on the floor.

Focus on an aspect of your breathing, such as the sensations of air flowing into your nostrils and out of your mouth, or your belly rising and falling as you inhale and exhale.

Once you've narrowed your concentration in this way, begin to widen your focus. Become aware of sounds, sensations, and your ideas.

Embrace and consider each thought or sensation without judging it good or bad. If your mind starts to race, return your focus to your breathing. Then expand your awareness again.

Learning to stay in the present

A less formal approach to mindfulness can also help you to stay in the present and fully participate in your life. You can choose any task or moment to practice informal mindfulness, whether you are eating, showering, walking, touching a partner, or playing with a child or grandchild.

Attending to these points will help:

Start by bringing your attention to the sensations in your body

Breathe in through your nose, allowing the air downward into your lower belly. Let your abdomen expand fully.

Now breathe out through your mouth

Notice the sensations of each inhalation and exhalation

Proceed with the task at hand slowly and with full deliberation

Engage your senses fully. Notice each sight, touch, and sound so that you savor every sensation.

When you notice that your mind has wandered from the task at hand, gently bring your attention back to the sensations of the moment.

Invest in yourself

The effects of mindfulness meditation tend to be dose-related — the more you do, the more effect it usually has. Most people find that it takes at least 20 minutes for the mind to begin to settle, so this is a reasonable way to start. If you're ready for a more serious commitment, Jon Kabat-Zinn recommends 45 minutes of meditation at least six days a week. But you can get started by practicing the techniques described here for shorter periods.

Moreover, mindfulness has also been found to have a positive impact on physical health, with studies suggesting that it can lower blood pressure, strengthen the immune system, and reduce the risk of various chronic diseases. By fostering a deep mind-body connection, mindfulness helps individuals develop a greater understanding of their own needs and promotes overall well-being.

In today's fast-paced and digitally connected world, the practice of mindfulness offers a powerful tool for individuals to navigate the complexities of life with greater clarity, presence, and compassion. By cultivating mindfulness, individuals can tap into their inner wisdom, find peace amidst the chaos, and live with a greater sense of purpose, authenticity, and joy. •

Whether incorporated as a daily practice, integrated into therapy, or used as a tool for personal growth, mindfulness has the potential to transform lives and create a more mindful, compassionate, and resilient society. By embracing the power of the present moment, individuals can embark on a transformative journey of self-discovery and find solace in the richness of the present, one breath at a time.

Mindfulness. It's a pretty straightforward word. It suggests that the mind is fully attending to what's happening, to what you're doing, to the space you're moving through. That might seem trivial, except for the annoying fact that we so often veer from the matter at hand. Our mind takes flight, we lose touch with our body, and pretty soon we're engrossed in obsessive thoughts about something that just happened or fretting about the future. And that makes us anxious.

Yet no matter how far we drift away, mindfulness is right there to snap us back to where we are and what we're doing and feeling. If you want to know what mindfulness is, it's best to try it for a while. Since it's hard to nail down in words, you will find slight variations in the meaning in books, websites, audio, and video.

When we think about mindfulness and meditating (with a capital M), we can get hung up on thinking about our thoughts: we're going to do something about what's happening in our heads. It's as if these bodies we have are just inconvenient sacks for our brains to lug around.

Having it all remain in your head, though, lacks a feeling of good old gravity. Meditation begins and ends in the body. It involves taking the time to pay attention to where we are and what's going on, and that starts with being aware of our body That approach can make it seem like floating—as though we don't have to walk. We can just waft.

The Basics of Mindfulness Practice

Mindfulness helps us put some space between ourselves and our reactions, breaking down our conditioned responses. Here's how to tune into mindfulness throughout the day:

Set aside some time. You don't need a meditation cushion or bench, or any sort of special equipment to access your mindfulness skills—but you do need to set aside some time and space. Observe the present moment as it is. The aim of mindfulness is not quieting the mind, or attempting to achieve a state of eternal calm. The goal is simple: we're aiming to pay attention to the present moment, without judgment. Easier said than done, we know. Let your judgments roll by. When we notice judgments arise during our practice, we can make a mental note of them, and let them pass. Return to observing the present moment as it is. Our minds often get carried away in thought. That's why mindfulness is the practice of returning, again and again, to the present moment. Be kind to your wandering mind. Don't judge yourself for whatever thoughts crop up, just practice recognizing when your mind has wandered off, and gently bring it back.

That's the practice. It's often been said that it's very simple, but it's not necessarily easy. The work is to just keep doing it. Results will accrue.

How to Really Listen

How often do you feel really listened to ? How often do you really listen to others ? (Be honest.)

We know we're in the presence of a good listener when we get that sweet, affirming feeling of really being heard. But sadly it occurs all too rarely. We can't force others to listen, but we can improve our own listening, and perhaps inspire others by doing so.

Good listening means mindful listening. Like mindfulness itself, listening takes a combination of intention and attention. The intention part is having a genuine interest in the other person—their experiences, views, feelings, and needs. The attention part is being able to stay present, open, and unbiased as we receive the other's words—even when they don't line up with our own ideas or desires.

Paradoxically, being good at listening to others requires the ability to listen to yourself. If you can't recognize your own beliefs and opinions, needs and fears, you won't have enough inner space to really hear anyone else. So the foundation for mindful listening is self-awareness.

Here are some tips to be a good listener to yourself so you can be a good listener for others.

How to Really Listen

1. Check inside: "How am I feeling just now? Is there anything getting in the way of being present for the other person?" If something is in the way, decide if it needs to be addressed first or can wait till later.

2. Feeling your own sense of presence, extend it to the other person with the intention to listen fully and openly, with interest, empathy, and mindfulness.

3. Silently note your own reactions as they arise—thoughts, feelings, judgments, memories. Then return your full attention to the speaker.

4. Reflect back what you are hearing, using the speaker's own words when possible, paraphrasing or summarizing the main point. Help the other person feel heard.

5. Use friendly, open-ended questions to clarify your understanding and probe for more. Affirm before you differ. Acknowledge the other person's point of view—acknowledging is not agreeing!—before introducing your own ideas, feelings, or requests.

How to Meditate

This meditation focuses on the breath, not because there is anything special about it, but because the physical sensation of breathing is always there and you can use it as an anchor to the present moment. Throughout the practice you may find yourself caught up in thoughts, emotions, sounds—wherever your mind goes, simply come back again to the next breath. Even if you only come back once, that's okay.

A Simple Meditation Practice

- Sit comfortably. Find a spot that gives you a stable, solid, comfortable seat.
- Notice what your legs are doing. If on a cushion, cross your legs comfortably in front of you. If on a chair, rest the bottoms of your feet on the floor.
- Straighten your upper body—but don't stiffen. Your spine has natural curvature. Let it be there.
- Notice what your arms are doing. Situate your upper arms parallel to your upper body. Rest the palms of your hands on your legs wherever it feels most natural.
- Soften your gaze. Drop your chin a little and let your gaze fall gently downward. It's not necessary to close your eyes. You can simply let what appears before your

eyes be there without focusing on it.

- Feel your breath. Bring your attention to the physical sensation of breathing: the air moving through your nose or mouth, the rising and falling of your belly, or your chest.

- Notice when your mind wanders from your breath. Inevitably, your attention will leave the breath and wander to other places. Don't worry. There's no need to block or eliminate thinking. When you notice your mind wandering gently return your attention to the breath.

- Be kind about your wandering mind. You may find your mind wandering constantly—that's normal, too. Instead of wrestling with your thoughts, practice observing them without reacting. Just sit and pay attention. As hard as it is to maintain, that's all there is. Come back to your breath over and over again, without judgment or expectation.

- When you're ready, gently lift your gaze (if your eyes are closed, open them). Take a moment and notice any sounds in the environment. Notice how your body feels right now. Notice your thoughts and emotions.

Mindful Practices for Every Day

As you spend time practicing mindfulness, you'll probably find yourself feeling kinder, calmer, and more patient. These shifts in your experience are likely to generate changes in other parts of your life as well.

Mindfulness can help you become more playful, maximize your enjoyment of a long conversation with a friend over a cup of tea, then wind down for a relaxing night's sleep.

What Is Mindfulness Meditation?

Mindfulness meditation is a mental training practice that teaches you to slow down racing thoughts, let go of negativity, and calm both your mind and body. It combines meditation with the practice of mindfulness, which can be defined as a mental state that involves being fully focused on "the now" so you can acknowledge and accept your thoughts, feelings, and sensations without judgment.

Techniques can vary, but in general, mindfulness meditation involves deep breathing and awareness of body and mind. Practicing mindfulness meditation doesn't require props or preparation (no need for candles, essential oils, or mantras, unless you enjoy them). To get started, all you need is a comfortable place to sit, three to five minutes of free time, and a judgment-free mindset.

How to Practice Mindfulness Meditation

Learning mindfulness meditation is straightforward enough to practice on your own, but a teacher or program can also help you get started, particularly if you're practicing meditation for specific health reasons. Here are some simple steps to help you get started on your own.

Remember, meditation is a practice, so it's never perfect. You are ready to begin now just as you are!

Get Comfortable

Find a quiet and comfortable place. Sit in a chair or on the floor with your head, neck, and back straight but not stiff. It's also helpful to wear comfortable, loose clothing so you're not distracted.

But being that this practice can be done anywhere for any amount of time, a dress code is not required.

The First Step in Meditation Is Finding a Comfortable Seat

Consider a Timer

While it's not necessary, a timer (preferably with a soft, gentle alarm) can help you focus on meditation and forget about time—and eliminate any excuses you have for stopping and doing something else.

Since many people lose track of time while meditating, it can also ensure you're not meditating for too long. Be sure to also allow yourself time after meditation to become aware of where you are and get up gradually.

While some people meditate for longer sessions, even a few minutes every day can make a difference. Begin with a short, 5-minute meditation session and increase your sessions by 10 or 15 minutes until you are comfortable meditating for 30 minutes at a time.

Focus on Breathing

Become aware of your breath, attuning to the sensation of air moving in and out of your body as you breathe. Feel your belly rise and fall as the air enters your nostrils and leaves your nostrils. Pay attention to the temperature change when the breath is inhaled versus when it's exhaled.

Notice Your Thoughts

The goal is not to stop your thoughts but to get more comfortable becoming the "witness" to the thoughts. When thoughts come up in your mind, don't ignore or suppress them. Simply note them, remain calm, and use your breathing as an anchor. Imagine your thoughts as clouds passing by; watch them float by as they shift and change.Repeat this as often as you need to while you are meditating.

Give Yourself a Break

If you find yourself getting carried away in your thoughts—whether with worry, fear, anxiety, or hope—observe where your mind went, without judgment, and just return to your breathing. Don't be hard on yourself if this happens; the practice of returning to your breath and refocusing on the present is the practice of mindfulness.

Download an App

If you're having trouble practicing mindfulness meditation on your own, consider downloading an app (like Calm or Headspace) that provides free meditations and teaches you a variety of tools to help you get centered throughout your day.

These 7 Apps Will Deepen Your Meditation Practice
Impact of Mindfulness Meditation

Regular practice of mindfulness meditation has benefits for your physical as well as your mental health. Some of these include:

Reducing stress: Mindfulness-based stress reduction (MBSR), a standardized therapeutic approach to mindfulness meditation, has been shown to reduce symptoms of stress in healthy individuals.[1] The practice has also been found to be beneficial for a number of mental and physical disorders including anxiety, depression, and chronic pain.

Lower heart rate: Heart disease is one of the top causes of death in the United States and research suggests that mindfulness may be beneficial for your heart. In one study, participants either enrolled in an online mindfulness meditation program or were added to a waitlist for traditional treatment for heart disease.[2] Those who participated in mindfulness meditation had significantly lower heart rates and performed better on a test of cardiovascular capacity.

Improved immunity: Research also suggests that mindfulness practices may improve your body's resistance to illness. One study compared the impact of both mindfulness and exercise on immune function.[3] They found that people who had taken part in an eight-week mindfulness course had greater gains in immune function than those in the exercise group.

Better sleep: Studies have also shown that practicing mindfulness meditation might improve sleep and even be useful for treating certain sleep disturbances. One 2019 study found that mindfulness meditation significantly improved sleep quality.

Making mindfulness meditation a regular practice can lead to stronger effects, but that doesn't necessarily mean that you need to do it every day. Studies have found that meditating three to four times per week can have big benefits—and, regularly meditating for eight weeks will actually alter the brain, according to neuroimaging studies.5

Tips to Practice Mindfulness in Daily Life

As you practice mindfulness meditation, it helps to find ways to bring mindfulness into your everyday life—especially on those days when life is too busy to carve out a minute alone. Mindfulness meditation is one technique, but everyday activities and tasks provide plenty of opportunities for mindfulness practice.

Brushing your teeth: Feel your feet on the floor, the brush in your hand, and your arm moving up and down.

Doing dishes: Savor the feeling of the warm water on your hands, the look of the bubbles, and the sounds of the pans clunking on the bottom of the sink.

Doing laundry: Pay attention to the smell of the clean clothes and the feel of the fabric. Add a focus element and count your breaths as you fold laundry.

Driving: Turn off the radio—or put on something soothing, like classical music. Imagine your spine growing tall, find the half-way point between relaxing your hands and gripping the wheel too tightly. Whenever you notice your mind wandering, bring your attention back to where you and your car are in space.

Exercising: Instead of watching television while on the treadmill, try focusing on your breathing and where your feet are as you move.

Getting started with a mindfulness meditation practice can sometimes seem intimidating, but it's important to remember that even a few minutes each day can be beneficial. Just a few minutes of being present can reap significant benefits. Even if you don't do it every day, it's a practice you can keep coming back to when you need it.

Mindfulness Based Cognitive Therapy (MBCT) is an evidence-based psychotherapeutic approach that was designed as a treatment for relapse prevention after repeated episodes of depression. MBCT was originally developed based on theoretical concepts about the origin of depression and potential mechanisms of relapse. One central idea in these concepts concerns cognitive reactivity as a risk factor for relapse of depression. In brief, in periods of low mood, negative thinking patterns that are associated with negative emotions and painful bodily sensations are thought to be reactivated automatically and may lead to relapse of depression by self-reinforcing cycles of ruminative thinking; this, in turn, is assumed to strengthen the association between dysphoria and depressogenic thinking and to increase the probability that ruminations are triggered in future episodes of low mood. In order to interrupt and prevent these processes, a core strategy of MBCT is the cultivation of mindfulness skills, derived from Buddhist traditions, which are supposed to target this self-perpetuating process.

The clinical efficacy of MBCT for preventing relapse after three or more depressive episodes has been demonstrated by multiple randomized control trials. By contrast, so far, the mechanisms and factors that mediate the effects of MBCT are not fully understood, nor whether these mechanisms match those of the theory behind MBCT. As for other psychotherapeutic approaches, a precise understanding of cognitive and neurophysiological mechanisms that mediate therapeutic effects are important in order to predict and optimize treatment outcomes, guide treatment selection for individual patients, and finesse existing therapeutic approaches.

There is no cheap and easy pathway to mental health and fulfillment, and critics are right to raise cautionary flags about mindfulness being a panacea. Nevertheless, mindfulness has caught on for good reasons, and there are genuine insights to be had. The point of this blog post is to help readers understand what mindfulness is and to provide a basic framework for how it works from the perspective of a unified view of human psychology.

Rooted in Buddhist traditions that emerged thousands of years ago, the modern mindfulness movement in the West was largely sparked by the work of Jon Kabat-Zinn, who developed Mindfulness-Based Stress Reduction (MBSR) programs at the University of Massachusetts Medical School, starting in 1979. His work was initially focused on helping patients deal with chronic pain. The problem was that patients would work to mentally escape or avoid the pain, but ultimately this inner struggle would create more problems and mental distress and exhaustion. By adopting a mindful approach to pain, Kabat-Zinn found he could relieve mental distress and improve functioning overall.

In the next decade or so, mindfulness became integrated into cognitive and behavioral approaches. Some prominent ones included approaches such as Marsha Linehan's Dialectical Behavior Therapy, Steve Hayes and colleagues' Acceptance and Commitment Therapy, and Segal and colleagues' Mindfulness-Based Cognitive Therapy.

But cognitive behavioral folks weren't the only ones paying attention to mindfulness. Richard Davidson's work in affective neuroscience forged a link between mindfulness and the brain. Mark Epstein's book, Thoughts Without a Thinker, offered an early bridge between mindfulness and a psychodynamic perspective. More recently, the interpersonal neurobiology movement led by individuals like Dan Siegel and Allan Schore offers an integrative, brain and attachment-based view of mental functioning that has mindfulness as a core principle. Emotion-focused perspectives, like that of Les Greenberg, also offer a perspective that is highly consistent with mindfulness-based teachings. Finally, the positive psychology movement, with its focus on growth and optimal functioning, has also raised the mindfulness banner.

"The secret to living happily is to love
deeply, to give generously, and to forgive
freely, knowing that love is the true source
of happiness."

CHAPTER SIX

Meditation with Anxiety

Anxiety is a common experience that many individuals face in their lives. The constant worry, racing thoughts, and physical sensations associated with anxiety can be overwhelming. Fortunately, meditation offers a powerful tool for managing anxiety and promoting emotional well-being. In this essay, we will explore the relationship between meditation and anxiety, delve into various meditation techniques, and discuss how meditation can cultivate inner peace and reduce anxiety symptoms.

Understanding Anxiety:

Anxiety is a natural response to perceived threats or stressors. It can manifest as excessive worry, restlessness, irritability, and physical symptoms such as rapid heartbeat or shortness of breath. While anxiety is a normal part of life, persistent and excessive anxiety can interfere with daily functioning and overall well-being.

The Benefits of Meditation for Anxiety:

Meditation has gained recognition as an effective practice for managing anxiety and promoting emotional well-being. Numerous studies have shown that regular meditation practice can reduce anxiety symptoms, improve emotional regulation, and enhance overall mental health. By calming the mind and cultivating present-moment awareness, meditation provides a sense of relief and allows individuals to develop a new relationship with their anxious thoughts and feelings.

Mindfulness Meditation:

Mindfulness meditation is a widely researched and practiced form of meditation that focuses on non-judgmental awareness of the present moment. It involves intentionally paying attention to thoughts, emotions, and physical sensations without getting caught up in them. Mindfulness meditation allows individuals to observe their anxiety from a place of detachment, reducing its impact on their well-being.

Deep Breathing Techniques:

Deep breathing techniques, such as diaphragmatic breathing or box breathing, can be powerful tools for managing anxiety. These techniques involve slow, deep breaths that engage the body's relaxation response, promoting a sense of calm and reducing anxiety symptoms. Incorporating deep breathing exercises into a meditation practice can help individuals regulate their breath and create a state of relaxation.

Loving-Kindness Meditation:

Loving-kindness meditation focuses on cultivating compassion and kindness towards oneself and others. By directing positive intentions and well-wishes towards oneself and others, individuals can counteract the self-critical and negative thought patterns often associated with anxiety. Loving-kindness meditation fosters self-acceptance, empathy, and a sense of connectedness, promoting emotional well-being.

Body Scan Meditation:

Body scan meditation involves systematically scanning the body and observing physical sensations without judgment. This practice cultivates body awareness and helps individuals develop a deeper understanding of the mind-body connection. By noticing tension, discomfort, or sensations associated with anxiety, individuals can bring compassionate attention to these areas and release physical and emotional tension.

Walking Meditation:

For individuals who find it challenging to sit still during meditation, walking meditation offers a viable alternative. Walking meditation involves focusing on the sensations of walking, the movement of the body, and the contact of the feet with the ground. This practice can be particularly beneficial for individuals with anxiety as it combines the benefits of physical activity with mindfulness, promoting relaxation and reducing anxiety symptoms.

Cultivating a Regular Meditation Practice:

Consistency is key when it comes to reaping the benefits of meditation for anxiety. Establishing a regular meditation practice, even for a few minutes a day, can have a profound impact on anxiety management. Setting aside a specific time and creating a comfortable meditation space can help individuals commit to their practice and make it a habit.

Integrating Meditation into Daily Life:

Meditation is not limited to formal sitting practice. It can be integrated into daily life to support anxiety management. Practicing mindful eating, incorporating brief moments of mindfulness throughout the day, or taking mini-meditation breaks during stressful situations can help individuals cultivate a sense of calm and presence amidst anxiety.

Mindfulness is the basic human ability to be fully present, aware of where we are and what we're doing, and not overly reactive or overwhelmed by what's going on around us.

Leading expert Jon Kabat-Zinn describes it as "awareness that arises through paying attention, on purpose, in the present moment, non-judgmentally," adding: "in the service of self-understanding and wisdom."

When you become aware of the present moment, you gain access to resources you may not have realized were with you all along—a stillness at your core. An awareness of what you need and don't need in your life that's with you all the time. You may not be able to change your situation, but mindfulness practice offers the space to change your response to your situation.

Mindfulness-Based Stress Reduction (MBSR), founded by Kabat-Zinn, the gold-standard for research-backed mindfulness. Developed over 40 years ago, MBSR is an 8-week program, including supported teachings, mindfulness practices, and movement practices that help people work with the stresses of everyday life. MBSR practices allow you to bring kind awareness and acknowledgment to any stressed or anxious feelings in your body and mind and simply allow them to be. A 1992 study in the American Journal of Psychiatry found that MBSR can effectively reduce symptoms of anxiety and panic even in those with generalized anxiety disorder, panic disorder, or panic disorder with agoraphobia.

According to other research, when you can create space between yourself and what you're experiencing, your anxiety can soften. But if you get too used to that low rumble of stress always being there, it can gradually grow, creating a stress "habit" that is detrimental to your health and well-being. Consequently, when we get caught up in patterns of reactivity, we create more distress in our lives. This is why it's so important to discern clearly the difference between reacting with unawareness and responding with mindfulness.

Mindfulness Works, But Not for Everyone

Meditation does seem to improve mental health—but it's not necessarily more effective than other steps you can take. Early research suggested that mindfulness meditation had a dramatic impact on our mental health. But as the number of studies has grown, so has scientific skepticism about these initial claims.

For example, a 2014 meta-analysis published in JAMA Internal Medicine examined 47 randomized controlled trials of mindfulness meditation programs, which included a total of 3,515 participants. They found that meditation programs resulted only in small to moderate reductions in anxiety and depression.

"In essence, practicing mindfulness is a process of learning to trust and stay with feelings of discomfort rather than trying to escape from or analyze them," says Bob Stahl, Ph.D., MBSR teacher, founder of multiple MBSR programs, and co-author of multiple books on MBSR. "This often leads to a remarkable shift; time and again your feelings will show you everything you need to know about them—and something you need to know for your own well-being.

How Mindfulness Calms Anxious Feelings

Mindfulness helps you learn to stay with difficult feelings without analyzing, suppressing, or encouraging them. When you allow yourself to feel and acknowledge your worries, irritations, painful memories, and other difficult thoughts and emotions, this often helps them dissipate.

Mindfulness allows you to safely explore the underlying causes of your stress and worry. By going with what's happening rather than expending energy fighting or turning away from it, you create the opportunity to gain insight into what's driving your concerns.

Mindfulness helps you create space around your worries so they don't consume you. When you begin to understand the underlying causes of your apprehension, freedom and a sense of spaciousness naturally emerge.

Calm Anxiety in Three Steps:

Open your attention to the present moment. The invitation is to bring attention to our experience in a wider and more open manner that isn't really involved with selecting or choosing or evaluating, but simply holding—becoming a container for thoughts, feelings or sensations in the body that are present and seeing if we can watch them from one moment to the next.

Focus on the breath. Let go of that widescreen and bring a focus that's much more concentrated and centered on breathing in one region of your body—the breath of the belly, or the chest, or the nostrils, or anywhere that the breath makes itself known, and keep that more concentrated focus.

Bring your attention to your body. Become aware of sensations in the body as a whole, sitting with the whole body, the whole breath, once again we move back to a wider and spacious container of attention for our experience.

The Science of Mindfulness Meditation for Anxiety

In 1992, Zindel Segal, John Teasdale, and Mark Williams collaborated to create an 8-week program modeled on Mindfulness-Based Stress Reduction (MBSR). Jon Kabat-Zinn—who developed MBSR—had some initial misgivings about the program, fearing the curriculum might insufficiently emphasize how important it is for instructors to have a deep personal relationship with mindfulness practice. Once he got to know the founders better, he became a champion for the program. In 2002, the three published Mindfulness-Based Cognitive Therapy for Depression: A New Approach to Preventing Relapse, now a landmark book.

MBCT's credibility rests firmly on ongoing research. Two randomized clinical trials (published in 2000 and 2008 in The Journal of Consulting and Clinical Psychology) laid the foundation, indicating MBCT reduces rates of depression relapse by 50% among patients who suffer from recurrent depression. Recent findings published in The Lancet in 2015 revealed that combining a tapering off of medication with MBCT is as effective as an ongoing maintenance dosage of medication. Further studies have found that MBCT is a potentially effective intervention for mood and anxiety disorders.

Should I Choose MBSR or MBCT?

According to the Centre for Mindfulness Studies, mindful awareness is the foundation of MBSR and MBCT. In both 8-week programs, participants are guided through a series of practices that encourage paying attention to experiences, thoughts, emotions, and sensations in the body. Explore the differences between MBSR and MBCT before you decide which program to follow.

Mindfulness-Based Cognitive Therapy:

Designed to prevent depressive relapse

Explores how mindfulness can help you stay well while dealing with depression or anxiety

Uses mindfulness practices to offer insight on negative mind states associated with depression and anxiety

Works to change your relationship to suffering by recognizing patterns in thought and emotion

Emphasizes your choice in how to respond to negative mind states

Recommended as an adjunctive treatment for unipolar depression and an intervention for symptoms of anxiety

How Mindfulness-Based Cognitive Therapy Helps with Anxiety

A skills-based approach, MBCT asks patients to inquire into, familiarize themselves with, and redirect the thought processes that are getting them into trouble (cognitive distortions, or what some people call "negative self-talk," or "stinkin' thinkin'"). It takes close attention and stick-to-itiveness to shift these ingrained thought processes. MBCT isn't about changing or fixing the content of our challenging thoughts, it's about becoming more intimately and consistently aware of these thoughts and patterns. The awareness itself reduces the grip of persistent and pernicious thought loops and storylines.

Like MBSR, MBCT is an eight-week program consisting of weekly two-hour classes with a mid-course day-long session. It combines guided meditations with group discussions, various kinds of inquiry and reflection, and take-home exercises. "Repetition and reinforcement, coming back to the same places, again and again, are key to the program," says Zindel Segal, "and hopefully people continue that into daily life beyond the initial MBCT program, in both good times and bad."

Can Mindfulness Really Help Reduce Anxiety?

A small study conducted at the University of Waterloo suggests that just 10 minutes of mindfulness helps with ruminative thought patterns. In the study, 82 participants who experience anxiety were given a computer task to complete, but were regularly disrupted. They were then split into two groups: one group listened to a guided meditation for 10 minutes, while the other group listened to an audio book for 10 minutes. Participants were then sent back to the computer while the disruptions continued.

The meditators had greater success in staying focused, and, as a result, they performed better on the task. "That was surprising to me," says lead researcher and psychology PhD candidate Mengran Xu. "Mindfulness meditation promoted a switch of attention from their internal thoughts to the external environment. It helped them focus on what's happening right now, in the moment, and not to get trapped in their worries."

This study adds to the growing body of evidence that mindfulness could be a powerful ally for people who struggle with ruminating thoughts and internal focus common with anxiety and depression. But, Xu adds, just why it helps is still unknown. "If we know how, we can make it more effective."

He wants to find out. Xu and colleagues have already finished one forthcoming study where participants were instructed in mindfulness meditation, muscle relaxation, or listened to an audio book. Xu says his team wants to see "how each intervention would affect people's scope of attention, cognition, and problem solving in a hypothetical stressful situation. The aim is to examine if mindfulness practice expands people's perspective.

"Sometimes [stress] is inevitable, but it depends on how broad your perspective is. Both mindfulness meditation, and relaxation can help broaden how people think about things."

"To love oneself is to embark on a lifelong journey of self-discovery and self-acceptance, embracing both the light and the shadow within."

CHAPTER SEVEN

Positive Relationships and Social Connections

Human beings are inherently social creatures, and our connections with others play a crucial role in shaping our well-being and overall quality of life. Positive relationships and social connections are essential for our emotional, mental, and physical health. In this essay, we will explore the significance of positive relationships, the benefits of social connections, and strategies for nurturing and fostering meaningful connections in our lives.

The Power of Positive Relationships:

Positive relationships encompass various connections, including family, friendships, romantic partnerships, and community bonds. These relationships have a profound impact on our well-being, influencing our happiness, self-esteem, resilience, and overall life satisfaction. Positive relationships provide emotional support, companionship, and a sense of belonging, creating a strong foundation for personal growth and fulfillment.

Social Connections and Health:

Numerous studies have shown that social connections are closely linked to our physical and mental health. Strong social ties have been associated with lower rates of depression, anxiety, and stress-related disorders. Social support can buffer the effects of life challenges, enhance our ability to cope with adversity, and promote faster recovery from illnesses. The quality of our relationships directly influences our overall health and longevity.

Building and Nurturing Positive Relationships:

Positive relationships do not happen by chance; they require effort, empathy, and effective communication. Building and nurturing positive relationships involve cultivating trust, open and honest communication, active listening, and empathy. It also entails mutual respect, kindness, and the willingness to invest time and energy in the relationship. Developing and maintaining positive relationships is an ongoing process that requires commitment and a genuine desire to connect with others.

Authentic Communication:

Authentic communication is the cornerstone of healthy relationships. It involves expressing oneself honestly, listening attentively, and responding with empathy. Authentic communication fosters trust, understanding, and emotional connection, allowing individuals to express their needs, emotions, and aspirations in a safe and supportive environment. By cultivating authentic communication, we can deepen our relationships and build a strong sense of connection.

Empathy and Compassion:

Empathy and compassion are essential qualities for fostering positive relationships. Empathy involves understanding and sharing another person's emotions, while compassion entails extending care, kindness, and support towards others. By practicing empathy and compassion, we create an atmosphere of understanding, validation, and mutual respect. These qualities enhance our relationships, promote emotional intimacy, and strengthen our social connections.

Cultivating Trust:

Trust is a vital component of positive relationships. Trust involves reliability, integrity, and a belief in the other person's goodwill. Building trust requires consistency, honesty, and keeping one's commitments. Trust creates a sense of safety and security within relationships, allowing individuals to be vulnerable, share their authentic selves, and develop deep bonds of connection.

Cultivating Social Connections:

Beyond individual relationships, cultivating social connections in the broader community is important for our well-being. Engaging in social activities, participating in group settings, and volunteering can provide opportunities for social interaction and a sense of belonging. Joining clubs, organizations, or community groups that align with our interests or values allows us to meet like-minded individuals and build social connections based on shared experiences.

The Role of Technology:

In the digital age, technology plays a significant role in connecting individuals and facilitating relationships. Social media platforms, online communities, and messaging apps provide avenues for staying connected and expanding our social networks. However, it's important to strike a balance and use technology in a way that enhances rather than replaces face-to-face interactions. Actively seeking in-person interactions and making time for offline connections is vital for cultivating deep and meaningful relationships.

Navigating Conflict and Building Resilience:

Conflict is a natural part of any relationship. Learning effective conflict resolution skills, practicing active listening, and seeking mutual understanding can help navigate conflicts and strengthen relationships. Building resilience within relationships involves embracing forgiveness, accepting imperfections, and adapting to changes and challenges together. Resilient relationships have the capacity to weather storms, grow stronger, and foster long-lasting connections.

Cultivating Self-Awareness and Self-Care:

Positive relationships are not solely dependent on external factors. Cultivating self-awareness and practicing self-care are crucial for nurturing healthy connections. By understanding our own needs, boundaries, and emotional well-being, we can communicate effectively and maintain a healthy balance in relationships. Engaging in self-care activities, prioritizing our own well-being, and fostering a positive relationship with ourselves provide a solid foundation for building and sustaining positive relationships with others.

Positive relationships and social connections are fundamental to our well-being and contribute to a fulfilling and flourishing life. They provide us with emotional support, a sense of belonging, and opportunities for growth and personal development. By cultivating authentic communication, empathy, trust, and resilience, we can foster deep and meaningful connections with others. Nurturing positive relationships not only enhances our own well-being but also contributes to a happier and more connected society.

Enjoying healthy and meaningful relationships and better social connection is essential for good mental and physical health.

As human beings we are hard wired to connect with each other; we are social beings and our family and community relationships give our lives purpose and meaning. Connecting with others not only helps us to survive but to thrive. And it is for this reason that BSLM prioritises the importance of healthy relationships as one of the six core pillars of lifestyle medicine.

From a physical health point of view there is a growing body of evidence demonstrating a link between the quality of our social connections and the associated risk of conditions including obesity, heart disease and even some cancers. Our mental health too is closely linked to our relationships with others, and loneliness is a key risk factor for depression.

Studies have calculated that loneliness can be as harmful to our health as smoking 15 cigarettes a day – or drinking at levels associated with alcoholism. High levels of loneliness can increase the risk of heart attack and strokes by 30 per cent.

BSLM believes that reducing loneliness and promoting social connection should therefore be a key part of the lifestyle medicine toolkit: connection truly is medicine.

A good lifestyle medicine practitioner must be ready to talk to their patient about loneliness, isolation and relationships. We should be ready to "prescribe connection" and offer help and advice on where and how people can meet others and feel less lonely and isolated. Here, social prescribing can be an incredibly powerful tool, and it's essential we have in place high quality networks which we can refer people into.

Lifestyle medicine practitioners should start by asking patients how much they see other people and where and how most of their social interactions take place. It's about discussing both the quantity as well as the quality of those relationships. In the consulting room, start by asking patients about their friendships, social networks and how much time they spend on their own or with others.

It's also important that we consider the many different opportunities for connection we can tap into: in the home, in the workplace, in our community, and in social groups and activities including sports and leisure.

Many of these networks have suffered because of the Covid-19 pandemic and associated lockdowns and restrictions which have reduced our ability to see family and friends and meet in groups. As we recover from the pandemic, BSLM believes we must act to rebuild these networks which play such a crucial role in our health and wellbeing.

Some aspects of our modern lifestyles are also acting to the detriment of our relationships and social connections. While the internet and social media can in some instances bring human beings together, it can also have the opposite effect. Spending long amounts of time on our screens and online cuts us off from people, reducing the amount of "face to face" time we spend with each other. Lifestyle medicine encourages and advocates for greater in person connection as the best way for us to reduce the risk of loneliness and isolation.

In summary: a lifestyle medicine approach to improving health and wellbeing should prioritise the importance of social connection and healthy relationships. These are critical to a lifestyle approach to healthy longevity alongside being active, a healthy diet, getting good quality sleep, avoiding harmful substances, and reducing stress.

HAVE YOU EVER WONDERED WHAT KEEPS US HEALTHY AND HAPPY AS WE GO THROUGH LIFE?

This question is what the researchers of one of the world's most prolonged studies, the Harvard Study of Adult Development, were trying to answer when they started their research in 1938. For decades, they tracked the lives of two different groups of men: Harvard sophomores and a group of boys from Boston's poorest neighborhoods.

They followed the lives of these 724 men from their teenage years through their '90s and, afterward, their children's lives. Every two years, they asked them to fill out some questionnaires, interviewed them at home, and even asked for access to their medical records. In 2015, Robert Waldinger, the fourth director of this Harvard 75 years study, shared their findings in a TED Talk that went viral. His most important message: having strong social connections and good relationships keeps us healthier and happier as we go through life.

SO, HOW CAN WE LIVE A HAPPY LIFE?

It turned out that the best predictor of who would grow into a happy, healthy octogenarian (someone who reaches age 80) at age 50 was not their cholesterol levels nor their blood pressure, but how satisfied they were in their relationships and having strong social connections. So, they realized that good relationships have a protective effect on our bodies and also on our brains since people in healthy relationships keep their memories sharper for longer.

Positive relationships are as crucial to physical, mental, and emotional well-being as eating healthy, exercising regularly, or getting enough sleep. Another landmark study showed that loneliness is a greater risk to our health than obesity, smoking, or high blood pressure. However, feeling lonely is always very personal. One can feel lonely while in a group or even in a long marriage, so the second big lesson is that it's not the quantity but the quality of our relationships that matter for strong connections. In fact, it is the quality of our relationships that determines the quality of our life.

WHY ARE STRONG SOCIAL CONNECTIONS SO GOOD FOR OUR HEALTH?

Studies show that strong social connections are linked to an increased chance of longevity, a better immune system, less inflammation, and faster recoveries from disease. When you feel more connected to others, you are less vulnerable to anxiety and depression and have higher self-esteem, empathy, and trust toward others. In other words, meaningful relationships generate a positive social, emotional, and physical well-being spiral. Unfortunately, the opposite is also true, and those who lack social connectedness are more prone to suffer a decline in physical and psychological health and are susceptible to becoming further isolated.

Our brains are hardwired for connection. We have both a biological and a psychological need for social support. Each time we genuinely connect with another person, we release the pleasure-inducing hormone oxytocin into the bloodstream, which reduces anxiety and improves concentration and focus.

Relationships are crucial for a whole and fulfilling life. But while most of us know how important relationships are for our happiness, we do not always live our life in accordance with this knowledge.

Building strong social connections can sometimes be challenging because human relationships are complicated and messy. Tending to family and friends is hard work and an effort that never ends. Some people find it hard to develop new friendships or keep up with existing ones. We are absorbed in our everyday life, overwhelmed with work or caring for children, and relationships can stop being a priority. Due to life changes, one can even grow apart from their old friends. Maybe you've moved to a new place and haven't yet met new people.

MAKING THE EFFORT OF HAVING STRONG SOCIAL CONNECTIONS IS TOTALLY WORTH IT

Developing and maintaining good relationships takes effort, but it's absolutely worth it. It is an investment that has the highest return in terms of what Dr. Tal Ben-Shahar, founder of the Happiness Studies Academy, calls the ultimate currency, which is happiness. To fulfill the potential latent in relationships, we need to make them a priority, and we need to make them real.

Happiness is a product of our pursuits — the pursuit of those things that make life worth living. Chris Peterson (1950-2012), one of the founding fathers of Positive Psychology, when asked what Positive Psychology was all about, used to say: «Other people matter. Anything that builds relationships between and among people is going to make you happy.»

Therefore, quality counts more than quantity. While research shows that it's good to cultivate a diversified network of friends because of the emotional variety that it provides us with, it's also important to nurture a few truly close friends who we can deeply trust and rely on.

WHAT CAN WE DO TO CULTIVATE MEANINGFUL RELATIONSHIPS?

Be proactive — reach out rather than wait for invitations to come your way, and do not be discouraged by a negative response. Keep trying. You may need to suggest plans a few times before everyone can commit.

Be curious, and ask what's going on in the other person's life. Let them know you care, make eye contact, and comments such as, «That sounds fun» or «I hear you.» Be empathetic, and don't give advice unless the other person asks for it.

Show that you can be trusted. Keep your engagements and follow through on commitments you've made. When someone shares confidential information with you, keep it private.

Be vulnerable. Willingness to disclose personal experiences and concerns shows that the other person holds a special place in your life, and this builds intimacy and deepens your connection.

Basically, strong social connections are the fabric of a good life but unlike love, friends are made rather than found. Therefore, we must build trust, have common interests and values, and spend time together if we want to grow meaningful connections.

WE CAN INCREASE OUR CHANCES OF MAKING NEW FRIENDS BY:

Joining a group or club that gathers around an interest or hobby you share.

Volunteering — Sharing a cause worth fighting for or helping others.

Practicing any team sport, like soccer or basketball.

Attending social gatherings.

Inviting a colleague to join you for coffee or lunch.

Going for a walk. Chatting with neighbors who are also out or starting conversations in the park.

So remember, it's never too late to build new relationships or reconnect with old friends. Investing time in making connections and strengthening your relationships always pays off in terms of the ultimate currency: happiness.

"In the cathedral of self-love, we celebrate
the sacredness of our own existence,
honoring the divine spark that dwells
within each of us."

CHAPTER EIGHT

Protecting Mental Health

In today's fast-paced and demanding world, preserving good mental health is vital for overall well-being and quality of life. While experiencing occasional stress, anxiety, or low mood is normal, it is essential to adopt strategies that promote mental well-being and help prevent the development of more serious mental health issues. This essay explores various strategies and practices that individuals can incorporate into their lives to avoid bad mental health and foster resilience.

Good mental health is essential for overall well-being and quality of life. It allows individuals to cope with stress, build positive relationships, and achieve their full potential. However, in today's fast-paced and challenging world, maintaining good mental health can be a struggle for many. This essay aims to provide a comprehensive guide on how to avoid bad mental health by exploring various strategies and practices that promote mental well-being. By understanding these techniques and incorporating them into daily life, individuals can develop resilience, manage stress effectively, and cultivate a positive mindset.

Understand Mental Health:

The first step in avoiding bad mental health is to understand what it means to have good mental health. Mental health is a continuum, ranging from thriving to experiencing mental health challenges. It is essential to recognize that everyone has mental health, just as they have physical health. Being aware of the signs of poor mental health and understanding when to seek help are critical aspects of maintaining well-being.

Promote Open Communication:

Open communication is fundamental to good mental health. Creating a safe and non-judgmental environment allows individuals to express their feelings, thoughts, and concerns without fear of stigma. Encouraging open communication within families, workplaces, and communities fosters understanding, support, and early detection of mental health issues.

Practice Self-Care:

Self-care is an essential aspect of maintaining good mental health. It involves taking intentional steps to nurture oneself physically, emotionally, and mentally. Self-care practices may include regular exercise, adequate sleep, maintaining a balanced diet, engaging in hobbies, spending time in nature, and setting healthy boundaries to protect mental well-being.

Develop Resilience:

Resilience is the ability to bounce back from adversity and cope with life's challenges effectively. Building resilience involves developing problem-solving skills, maintaining a positive outlook, and learning from difficult experiences. Engaging in mindfulness practices and seeking social support can also enhance resilience.

Prioritize Mental Health at Work:

Work-related stress and burnout can significantly impact mental health. Prioritizing mental health in the workplace involves fostering a supportive and inclusive environment, providing access to resources like employee assistance programs, and promoting work-life balance. Employers can also implement stress reduction programs and encourage open conversations about mental health.

Limit Exposure to Negativity:

Constant exposure to negative news, social media, or toxic relationships can have adverse effects on mental health. Setting boundaries and limiting exposure to negativity can significantly improve mental well-being. Instead, focus on positive and uplifting content, cultivate positive relationships, and practice gratitude to shift the focus to the good in life.

Engage in Regular Physical Activity:

Physical activity is not only beneficial for physical health but also has a positive impact on mental well-being. Regular exercise releases endorphins, which are natural mood-boosting chemicals. Engaging in physical activity can reduce stress, anxiety, and symptoms of depression while promoting a sense of accomplishment and self-esteem.

Seek Social Support:

Social connections play a crucial role in maintaining good mental health. Seek support from friends, family, or support groups during challenging times. Sharing experiences and emotions with others can provide validation and comfort, reducing feelings of isolation and loneliness.

Practice Mindfulness and Meditation:

Mindfulness and meditation practices can improve mental well-being by promoting present-moment awareness and reducing rumination. Mindfulness techniques help individuals focus on the here and now, promoting a sense of calm and reducing stress. Regular meditation can enhance self-awareness, regulate emotions, and improve overall mental resilience.

Seek Professional Help When Needed:

Recognizing when professional help is needed is essential for avoiding bad mental health. If symptoms persist, interfere with daily functioning, or cause significant distress, seeking help from a mental health professional is vital. Therapy, counseling, and medication can be valuable tools in managing mental health challenges.

Avoiding bad mental health requires intentional effort and a commitment to self-care and well-being. By understanding the importance of mental health, practicing self-care, managing stress effectively, seeking social support, and implementing strategies like mindfulness and resilience-building, individuals can foster good mental health and reduce the risk of negative outcomes. Remember, good mental health is a lifelong journey, and it is essential to prioritize self-care and seek help when needed. By adopting these strategies and integrating them into daily life, individuals can promote their mental well-being and lead happier and more fulfilling lives.

Self-care is the foundation of good mental health. It involves engaging in activities that nurture and support your overall well-being. Here are some key aspects of self-care:

Physical health: Maintain a balanced and nutritious diet, engage in regular exercise, get enough sleep, and limit substances like alcohol and tobacco.

Stress management: Develop healthy coping mechanisms for stress, such as practicing mindfulness, deep breathing exercises, and engaging in relaxation techniques like yoga or meditation.

Time for yourself: Carve out regular periods for activities you enjoy, hobbies, and personal interests. Allow yourself time to relax and unwind.

Resilience is the ability to bounce back from adversity and cope with life's challenges. Strengthening resilience can help prevent the negative impact of stress on mental health. Consider the following strategies:

Develop a growth mindset: Embrace challenges as opportunities for growth and learning rather than as obstacles. Cultivate a belief in your ability to overcome difficulties.

Seek support: Build a network of supportive relationships with family, friends, or professionals. Reach out for help when needed, as social support is crucial for resilience.

Foster optimism: Practice positive thinking and reframing negative situations. Focus on solutions rather than dwelling on problems.

Practice self-compassion: Treat yourself with kindness, understanding, and acceptance. Be mindful of your self-talk and practice self-compassion during difficult times.

Setting and maintaining healthy boundaries is essential for protecting your mental health. Boundaries help define what is acceptable and comfortable for you in relationships, work, and other areas of life. Consider the following:

Learn to say no: Respectfully decline requests or commitments that exceed your capacity or compromise your well-being.

Identify your limits: Understand your emotional, physical, and mental limits and communicate them clearly to others.

Protect your time and energy: Prioritize activities and relationships that align with your values and contribute positively to your well-being.

Practice assertiveness: Express your needs, thoughts, and feelings in a direct and respectful manner.

Stress can significantly impact mental health if left unmanaged. Implementing effective stress management techniques is crucial for maintaining good mental well-being. Consider the following strategies:

Time management: Prioritize tasks, break them down into manageable steps, and establish a schedule that allows for breaks and self-care.

Relaxation techniques: Engage in activities that promote relaxation, such as deep breathing exercises, progressive muscle relaxation, or engaging in hobbies.

Healthy coping mechanisms: Instead of turning to unhealthy coping mechanisms like excessive alcohol consumption or avoidance, find healthy outlets for stress, such as exercise, creative pursuits, or talking to a supportive friend or professional.

Positive social connections play a significant role in maintaining good mental health. Building and nurturing meaningful relationships can provide support, a sense of belonging, and promote positive emotions. Consider the following:

Foster healthy relationships: Surround yourself with positive and supportive individuals who uplift you and encourage your growth.

Cultivate social connections: Engage in activities and join groups or communities that align with your interests and values.

Practice active listening: Show genuine interest in others and practice active listening skills. Maintain open and honest communication.

If you experience persistent or worsening symptoms of poor mental health, it is crucial to seek professional help. Mental health professionals can provide appropriate diagnosis, treatment, and support. Remember that seeking help is a sign of strength and a proactive step towards better mental well-being.

Avoiding bad mental health requires a proactive approach that incorporates self-care, building resilience, establishing healthy boundaries, managing stress effectively, nurturing relationships, and seeking professional help when needed. By implementing these strategies and making mental health a priority, individuals can reduce the risk of developing mental health issues and foster a sense of well-being, resilience, and overall happiness. Remember, taking care of your mental health is a lifelong journey that requires dedication, self-awareness, and a commitment to prioritizing your well-being.

Mental health includes our emotional, psychological, and social well-being. It affects how we think, feel, and act as we cope with life. It also helps determine how we handle stress, relate to others, and make choices. Mental health is important at every stage of life, from childhood and adolescence through adulthood and aging.

Why is mental health important?

Mental health is important because it can help you to:

Cope with the stresses of life

Be physically healthy

Have good relationships

Make meaningful contributions to your community

Work productively

Realize your full potential

How can I improve my mental health?

There are many different things you can do to improve your mental health, including:

Staying positive. It's important to try to have a positive outlook; some ways to do that include:

Finding balance between positive and negative emotions. Staying positive doesn't mean that you never feel negative emotions, such as sadness or anger. You need to feel them so that you can move through difficult situations. They can help you to respond to a problem. But you don't want those emotions to take over. For example, it's not helpful to keep thinking about bad things that happened in the past or worry too much about the future.

Trying to hold on to the positive emotions when you have them

Taking a break from negative information. Know when to stop watching or reading the news. Use social media to reach out for support and feel connected to others but be careful. Don't fall for rumors, get into arguments, or negatively compare your life to others.

Practicing gratitude, which means being thankful for the good things in your life. It's helpful to do this every day, either by thinking about what you are grateful for or writing it down in a journal. These can be big things, such as the support you have from loved ones, or little things, such as enjoying a nice meal. It's important to allow yourself a moment to enjoy that you had the positive experience. Practicing gratitude can help you to see your life differently. For example, when you are stressed, you may not notice that there are also moments when you have some positive emotions. Gratitude can help you to recognize them.

Taking care of your physical health, since your physical and mental health are connected. Some ways to take care of your physical health include:

Being physically active. Exercise can reduce feelings of stress and depression and improve your mood.

Getting enough sleep. Sleep affects your mood. If you don't get a good sleep, you may become more easily annoyed and angry. Over the long term, a lack of quality sleep can make you more likely to become depressed. So it's important to make sure that you have a regular sleep schedule and get enough quality sleep every night.

Healthy eating. Good nutrition will help you feel better physically but could also improve your mood and decrease anxiety and stress. Also, not having enough of certain nutrients may contribute to some mental illnesses. For example, there may be a link between low levels of vitamin B12 and depression. Eating a well-balanced diet can help you to get enough of the nutrients you need.

Connecting with others. Humans are social creatures, and it's important to have strong, healthy relationships with others. Having good social support may help protect you against the harms of stress. It is also good to have different types of connections. Besides connecting with family and friends, you could find ways to get involved with your community or neighborhood. For example, you could volunteer for a local organization or join a group that is focused on a hobby you enjoy.

Developing a sense of meaning and purpose in life. This could be through your job, volunteering, learning new skills, or exploring your spirituality.

Developing coping skills, which are methods you use to deal with stressful situations. They may help you face a problem, take action, be flexible, and not easily give up in solving it.

Meditation, which is a mind and body practice where you learn to focus your attention and awareness. There are many types, including mindfulness meditation and transcendental meditation. Meditation usually involves:

A quiet location with as few distractions as possible

A specific, comfortable posture. This could be sitting, lying down, walking, or another position.

A focus of attention, such as a specially chosen word or set of words, an object, or your breathing

An open attitude, where you try to let distractions come and go naturally without judging them

Relaxation techniques are practices you do to produce your body's natural relaxation response. This slows down your breathing, lowers your blood pressure, and reduces muscle tension and stress. Types of relaxation techniques include:

Progressive relaxation, where you tighten and relax different muscle groups, sometimes while using mental imagery or breathing exercises

Guided imagery, where you learn to focus on positive images in your mind, to help you feel more relaxed and focused

Biofeedback, where you use electronic devices to learn to control certain body functions, such as breathing, heart rate, and muscle tension

Self-hypnosis, where the goal is to get yourself into a relaxed, trance-like state when you hear a certain suggestion or see a specific cue

Deep breathing exercises, which involve focusing on taking slow, deep, even breaths

It's also important to recognize when you need to get help. Talk therapy and/or medicines can treat mental disorders. If you don't know where to get treatment, start by contacting your primary care provider.

"To be carefree is to dance through life's challenges with a lightness of being, embracing the present moment with joy and spontaneity."

CHAPTER NINE

The Pursuit of Meaning and Purpose

Human beings have an innate desire to find meaning and purpose in their lives. The pursuit of meaning goes beyond material wealth and superficial achievements, as it encompasses a deeper sense of fulfillment and significance. In this essay, we will explore the importance of meaning and purpose, the benefits of living a purpose-driven life, and strategies for discovering and nurturing a sense of meaning in our daily existence.

Understanding Meaning and Purpose:

Meaning refers to the significance and value we ascribe to our lives and experiences. It involves finding a sense of purpose, connection, and coherence in our actions and endeavors. Purpose, on the other hand, is the overarching direction or goal that gives our lives a sense of direction and meaning. Meaning and purpose intertwine to provide us with a sense of fulfillment and a reason to wake up each day with enthusiasm.

The Significance of Meaning and Purpose:

Living a life infused with meaning and purpose has numerous benefits for our overall well-being. It gives us a sense of direction and clarity, which helps us make decisions aligned with our values and aspirations. Meaning and purpose provide motivation, fueling our persistence and resilience in the face of challenges. They enhance our sense of self-worth and contribute to higher levels of happiness and life satisfaction.

Discovering Personal Values and Passions:

Understanding our personal values and passions is a crucial step in uncovering meaning and purpose. Reflecting on what truly matters to us, the activities that bring us joy and fulfillment, and the impact we want to have in the world helps us align our actions with our core values. Identifying our passions allows us to pursue activities and goals that bring a deep sense of satisfaction and meaning.

Setting Meaningful Goals:

Setting meaningful goals is instrumental in cultivating a sense of purpose. Meaningful goals are those that resonate with our values, ignite our passion, and contribute to our growth and well-being. These goals provide a sense of direction and a framework for our actions, enabling us to channel our energy towards pursuits that matter to us. By setting and pursuing meaningful goals, we give our lives purpose and a sense of accomplishment.

Finding Meaning in Work:

Work takes up a significant portion of our lives, and finding meaning in our professional endeavors is crucial for overall well-being. Meaningful work involves aligning our skills, talents, and passions with a larger purpose or mission. It may involve contributing to a cause we care deeply about, making a positive impact on others, or using our skills to bring about positive change in the world. Finding meaning in our work gives us a sense of fulfillment and allows us to experience joy and satisfaction in our professional lives.

Cultivating Meaningful Relationships:

Meaningful relationships play a pivotal role in our pursuit of meaning and purpose. Connecting with others on a deep and authentic level provides us with a sense of belonging, support, and shared experiences. Building and nurturing meaningful relationships involve fostering empathy, compassion, and genuine connections. Meaningful relationships give us opportunities for growth, learning, and a sense of being part of something larger than ourselves.

Embracing Mindfulness and Gratitude:

Mindfulness and gratitude are powerful practices that can enhance our experience of meaning and purpose. Mindfulness involves being fully present in the moment, appreciating the richness of each experience, and finding meaning in the ordinary. Gratitude helps us focus on the positive aspects of our lives and cultivates a sense of appreciation for the simple joys and blessings. By embracing mindfulness and gratitude, we deepen our understanding of the meaningful aspects of our lives.

Giving Back and Contributing to Others:

Contributing to the well-being of others is a meaningful way to find purpose in our lives. Acts of kindness, volunteering, or engaging in philanthropy allow us to make a positive impact on the lives of others, creating a ripple effect of positivity and meaning. Giving back not only benefits those we help but also nourishes our own sense of purpose and fulfillment.

Embracing Personal Growth and Lifelong Learning:

Personal growth and lifelong learning are integral to the pursuit of meaning and purpose. Engaging in continuous self-improvement, seeking new experiences, and expanding our knowledge and skills contribute to our sense of fulfillment and personal development. Embracing challenges, stepping out of our comfort zones, and being open to new perspectives foster growth and enrich our journey towards meaning and purpose.

Embracing Transcendent Experiences:

Transcendent experiences, such as engaging in spiritual practices, connecting with nature, or exploring artistic expressions, can provide a profound sense of meaning and purpose. These experiences allow us to transcend our individual selves and connect with something greater than ourselves. Engaging in activities that evoke awe, wonder, and a sense of interconnectedness can deepen our understanding of the world and our place within it.

The pursuit of meaning and purpose is a lifelong journey that requires introspection, self-discovery, and conscious choices. By aligning our actions with our values, setting meaningful goals, cultivating meaningful relationships, embracing mindfulness and gratitude, contributing to others, seeking personal growth, and engaging in transcendent experiences, we can navigate a life filled with purpose and fulfillment. Finding meaning and purpose brings depth, joy, and a profound sense of satisfaction to our lives, allowing us to live authentically and make a positive impact on the world around us.

Inthe vast expanse of human existence, the pursuit of purpose has always been a focal point of contemplation and introspection. From the earliest philosophers to the modern-day seekers, the question of "Finding Your Purpose in Life" has ignited the flames of curiosity and propelled individuals on profound journeys of self-discovery. It is a quest that transcends the boundaries of time and space, delving into the depths of human consciousness and probing the mysteries of our existence.

At its essence, the search for purpose is an existential inquiry into the fundamental nature of being. It is a quest to unearth the raison d'être that underpins our existence, to discern the significance of our fleeting moments in the vast expanse of the universe. Yet, in our modern world, characterized by its frenetic pace and relentless pursuit of material gain, the pursuit of purpose often takes a backseat to the demands of daily life. We find ourselves caught in a perpetual cycle of busyness, chasing after external validations and fleeting pleasures, while the deeper questions of meaning and purpose linger in the background, awaiting our attention.

To set out on the journey of "Finding Your Purpose in Life" is to venture on a voyage of self-discovery, introspection, and transformation. It requires a willingness to peel back the layers of societal conditioning and cultural expectations, to confront the shadows lurking within our psyche, and to embrace the uncertainty and ambiguity that accompany the quest for meaning. It is a journey that demands courage, resilience, and an unwavering commitment to authenticity and truth.

In our search for purpose, we often look outward for guidance and validation, seeking affirmation from external sources and measuring our worth against societal standards of success and achievement. Yet, true purpose can never be found in the external world; it resides within the depths of our own being, waiting to be discovered and nurtured. It is a flame that flickers within us, guiding us on our journey and illuminating the path ahead.

The pursuit of purpose is not a linear journey but rather a meandering odyssey marked by twists and turns, setbacks and breakthroughs. It is a process of trial and error, of exploration and discovery, as we navigate the labyrinthine pathways of our own consciousness. Along the way, we encounter moments of doubt and uncertainty, moments of clarity and insight, each serving to deepen our understanding of ourselves and our place in the world.

In our quest for purpose, we must confront the existential void that lies at the heart of human existence. We must grapple with the inherent absurdity of life, the inevitability of our mortality, and the fleeting nature of our existence. It is in the face of these existential truths that we are compelled to search for meaning, to create purpose, and to imbue our lives with significance.

The search for purpose is not a solitary endeavor but rather a communal pursuit, woven into the fabric of our interconnectedness with all beings. It is a recognition that our individual destinies are intricately linked to the collective unfolding of humanity, that our lives are but threads in the tapestry of existence. It is a call to action, a summons to contribute our unique gifts and talents to the greater good, and to leave a lasting legacy that transcends the boundaries of time and space.

In addition, "Finding Your Purpose in Life" is a deeply personal and subjective endeavor, shaped by our unique experiences, perspectives, and aspirations. It is a journey of self-discovery, self-realization, and self-actualization, in which we come to know ourselves more fully and to live authentically in alignment with our deepest values and aspirations.

As we navigate the winding pathways of existence, let us remember that purpose is not something to be found but rather something to be created. Let us embrace the inherent uncertainty of life, the beauty of impermanence, and the infinite possibilities that lie before us. Let us heed the call of our innermost selves and venture on the journey of "Finding Your Purpose in Life" with courage, curiosity, and an open heart. Additionally, "Finding Your Purpose in Life" is a deeply personal and subjective endeavor, shaped by our unique experiences, perspectives, and aspirations. It is a journey of self-discovery, self-realization, and self-actualization, in which we come to know ourselves more fully and to live authentically in alignment with our deepest values and aspirations.

Lastly, it is not the destination that matters but the journey itself, the moments of joy and sorrow, of triumph and defeat, that shape us into who we are. And in that journey, may we find meaning, purpose, and fulfillment beyond measure.

"In the tapestry of life, every thread—joy and sorrow, triumph and tribulation—contributes to the beauty of the whole."

CHAPTER TEN

The Power of Sustainable Self-Care

Have you ever pruned or cut back a tree or a plant, then been shocked at how barren it looks? Only to then watch with amazement as each branch explodes with new life? I used to be reluctant to cut back any plant until someone told me that it is actually good for plants.

It goes against everything that we think is "healthy." How could inflicting such trauma and stress help plants grow and, yes, even thrive? This is just a simple example of nature's fight for survival. When we prune the plant or tree, it then puts even greater energy into growing more. Having been hacked to pieces, plants and trees could decide to give in, to just shrivel up and die. But they don't. The same is true for us. When things get tough, we can choose: to give in or to give more, to get bitter or to get better. We can choose to mirror nature and face our problems rather than run from them. We can choose to meet the stressors we are facing and use them to help us expand our capacity for resilience, and perhaps even thrive as a result.

One morning, during a particularly difficult time in my life, I was lying on the floor, scared about the future, and I thought about the blessings of this challenge. I thought about the line in Mary Oliver's poem "The Uses of Sorrow": "Someone I loved once gave me a box full of darkness. It took me years to understand that this too, was a gift." At that time, in my box full of darkness were the fossilized remains of a failed marriage, but I also had my son. My physical body was failing me, but it was also asking me to take note and remember to appreciate my health. My mental condition was frightening me, but it also presented an opportunity for me to step into courage. My life had been dictated for so long by other people and forces—my parents, my husband, my religion, societal norms—and now I was free to make my own decisions. This was my reckoning to choose, and I was consciously going to lean in to it. I knew that change is one of the only certain things in our lives, and so I had that choice to make. I wanted to get better, and I knew that required me to give more.

I wanted to try and accept this box of darkness and see it as a positive thing, a gift, as much as possible. What got me through this turbulent time was writing my own self-care list.

Why Self-Care Feels Selfish

Self-care means we commit to taking an active role in safeguarding our mental and physical wellness, proactively and (especially) in times of duress.

By definition, self-care means doing what is good for us—increasing our emotional and physical stamina, improving our self-esteem, and building resilience. Maintaining good self-care ensures that we stay compassionate, impassioned, and engaged. It means doing important work in one area without sacrificing other parts of our life. It means maintaining a positive attitude in spite of personal challenges and the larger injustices in the world. Self-care activities create daily improvement in our lives and have beneficial long-term effects. That said, these activities are not always fun. Sometimes they even border on boring.

Self-care means doing what is good for us—increasing our emotional and physical stamina, improving our self-esteem, and building resilience.

We might feel guilty about self-care because it can go against what we've been taught, which is that to be a good friend, parent, spouse or partner, coworker, and community member we have to put others first. Self-care means putting ourselves first, and we're often conditioned to believe this is wrong. It's rude. It isn't consistent with how so many inspirational leaders throughout history are portrayed, such as Gandhi, Nelson Mandela, Martin Luther King Jr., Susan B. Anthony, and Margaret Sanger. We admire these individuals because they endured suffering and hardship, while practicing self-sacrifice. Proper nutrition, healthy relationships, and exercise are secondary, if not frivolous. They didn't have time for yoga!

Two problems contribute to a negative view of self-care. The first is what I mention above, that self-care is often considered self-centered. It can imply caring that extends only to ourselves as individuals. But we can expand our definition of self to extend beyond the individual and include our family, community, the natural world, and all sentient beings. Self-care actually means caring for the entire community of which we are a part; it encompasses and protects this larger order. Self-care is not about being virtuous. In a way, it means living and working in ways that are consistent with and model how we want the world to work.

Additionally, the concept of self-care has been hijacked by corporations to create a profitable industrial wellness complex, one that focuses on beauty, happiness, and comfort in the name of self-love and self-compassion. In Western society, this is mostly geared toward white women of means, but it can include anyone. The main goal of this industry is to sell goods and services that provide only a superficial appearance of self-care, one that is often, in fact, indulgent and frivolous precisely because it's a temporary quick fix that only aims to make the individual feel better about themselves.

We can expand our definition of self to extend beyond the individual and include our family, community, the natural world, and all sentient beings.

The reality is that authentic self-care is unsexy, hard work—which isn't an attractive marketing pitch for corporations or brands. The way the term is broadly used today has very little to do with the healthy choices that reflect true self-love and self-compassion. It certainly has nothing to do with the struggle to survive in the face of political and structural oppression. For communities that are under attack by their own government, and for individuals with little access to health care, fresh food, clean water, and safe housing, self-care is a radical act of self-preservation.

What is Authentic Self-Care?

Authentic self-care is for everyone. It's what we all need and deserve, but it can be hard because it's not a quick fix. Ironically, neither is our own inner journey, or something as lofty as social justice work. Seen this way, wellness is one aspect of social justice, and like social justice, wellness doesn't happen overnight.

This is another reason that self-care has gotten such a bad name: It is much easier to practice "self-care" in easy ways that feel good right now than it is to develop the discipline of a healthy lifestyle that often sucks in the moment but feels really great later. Authentic self-care is not self-indulgence. Self-indulgence is unrestrained gratification of our desires and whims, behaviors meant only to alter our mood and provide a m temporary escape from pain and grief

How can we tell the difference between self-indulgence and true acts of self-care? First, ask if what you're doing is a temporary quick fix or something that is meant to yield long-term benefits. Sometimes, self-care is best expressed by setting limits in ways that prioritize what's most important. This takes discipline. Some everyday examples might include watching only one episode of a TV show, not bingeing a whole season, so you get to bed at a decent hour and experience a full night's rest. It might be not having a glass of wine with dinner, or only having one; saying no when you don't want to do some- thing; or waking up early so you have extra time to meditate, journal, or exercise before work.

The morning when I wrote my own self-care list, which was my response to true despair and a will to survive, I felt an instinctual inner knowing that I had to give up most of my vices in order to truly dedicate myself to self-care, to my healing, and to my overall wellness. If the work we do in the world is larger than ourselves—I knew there were healthy indulgences I could still enjoy, ones that provided important moments of joy and happiness. For me, these were defined by even the smallest of actions that helped me restore balance during one of the most imbalanced periods in my life. This included things like spending an evening reading a good book with a mud mask on my face, shutting down my phone and not respond- ing to texts or emails for a few hours of solitude, and having a meal with a friend while engaging in meaningful conversation. I didn't consider any of these things frivolous.

My point is this: Self-care is not one-size-fits-all. We each must decide what's right for ourselves. The biggest challenge I needed to overcome was the guilt and ingrained belief that taking any time for myself was selfish. In the end, what I learned from this experience is that tending to myself is a way to reaffirm that I value myself, and because I do, I must also honor myself. Taking that time to reaffirm in writing that "I am not broken" set me on my path and positioned me front and center as my own cheer- leader and self-advocate. Yet I can also proclaim irrefutably that authentic self-care is a truly selfless act—one that made me into a healthier being, a more engaged mother, and eventually, an impassioned self-care activist.

What Does a Sustainable Self-Care Regimen Look Like?

It doesn't look like a list of New Year's resolutions. Most of those never get kept. Just because I wrote down a list of things that I knew should be the cornerstone of my "self-care plan" didn't mean I suddenly enacted everything without fail from then on. I failed miserably, in fact. Following through was incredibly difficult. There were days I didn't seek support or get exercise; days when I ate and drank things I knew would increase my inflammation. I didn't always create healthy boundaries with others. Oftentimes I took on more than I should have. My lingering guilt over being a single mom and my need to please people in order to amplify my self-worth didn't vanish. Eventually, though, by not beating myself up for these infractions and by giving myself permission to begin anew each day—coupled with putting in place the most critical component of all, a community of care—I was able to develop a self-care rhythm.

Through this trial and error, I learned that, to be sustainable, a self-care plan needs to be gentle enough to work. It has to be incremental and composed of a lot of little things. Self-care might start as a set of promises we make to ourselves, but to enact them, we need to find a rhythm we can live with. Like a musical rhythm, a self-care rhythm is a regular, repeated pattern of actions that helps maintain the song of our life. That is, this rhythm is integrated into and supports whatever we are already doing on a daily basis. It's not a disruption. Rather, it enhances our life.

There are actually four self-care rhythms we can focus on: daily, weekly, seasonally, and annually. Getting into a new self-care groove wasn't easy at first. Like most people, I have a hard time creating and maintaining a balance between work, social life, family, and other obligations. Every evening and on the weekends, I would take my work home with me, whether it was task-related work (such as paperwork or answering emails) or emotional work (bearing the burdens of my community or clients). Of course, I couldn't entirely stop bringing work home at times (who can?), but I needed to establish a more formal separation between work and my personal space.

One of the ways that helped me create a better work-life balance was to identify the mudrooms in my life, so to speak. Just like a home's entryway, I developed formal transition rituals or practices that allowed me to shift from my public self to my personal self. Over time, these micro-practices became healthy habits that contributed to my overall self-care. For example, on my commute home, I practiced mindful driving in silence instead of taking phone calls or listening to talk radio.

To achieve a weekly rhythm, I wanted to balance my activities between four different areas that I identified: work, family and relationships, "me time," and my cultural traditions. Every week, I tried to be conscious about making sure that each of these areas was getting enough of my time and that they were balanced in ways that provided me energy and nourishment. Then, I looked at longer stretches of time and considered each season and each year and asked: Was I providing for all my needs on a regular, ongoing basis? This took careful scrutiny and constant adjustment. Not every day, week, season, or year is the same, and I never found a perfect balance or formula that worked all the time.

Making Room for Sustainable Self-Care

Consider the rhythms of your daily life—what would qualify as your mudrooms? What physical spaces or natural pauses already exist that would allow you to transition more elegantly from one demand or obligation to another? What about the weekly balance of your activities? Are some areas of your life being overrun or overwhelmed by others? You are the architect of your life, so consider your whole house and how to change things so that you can function at your best.

As you do this, one thing you might realize is that your home might be nice and fulfilling to live in if it wasn't so full of clutter, if it wasn't in such disarray. Every home has a junk drawer or two, along with a hallway closet or room where we shove things when guests come over to hide our clutter. We may fool our guests, but the clutter remains once they leave, and it inevitably spills over and grows. Mudrooms are like magnets for clutter—full of carelessly strewn shoes and boots, rain jackets and winter coats, single gloves without a matching pair, duffel bags filled with equipment and uniforms, and even bags of new but unused items that, despite our good intentions, are still waiting to be returned to the store even after months and months. The problem with this chaotic scene is that the mayhem eventually becomes an obstacle, a literal physical boundary preventing us from entering or exiting our home. Before leaving the house, we waste time pawing through this minefield looking for the "other" shoe or that matching glove. What can undo this madness? A team effort, of course. We need to take a community approach to the common cause of self-care.

Despite my efforts and best-laid plans—writing down and chunking my self-care activities, focusing on mudrooms and building smaller habits—I still consistently fell short of my goals. I couldn't adhere to my self-care plan because I was constantly tripping over my own clutter.

Creating a Community of Care

Eventually, all the women in my life who had become my support system were the ones who helped me get this mess in order. These women were friends who became sisters; some were only acquaintances when I was married but became my safety net once I was a single mom. Ultimately, this group of individuals became my formal "community of care," and they were exactly what I needed in order to fulfill my obligations to myself.

My Aunt Mrs. Jyoti helped me realize this epiphany one day as I was venting to her about how I had no time or energy left at the end of every night to take care of even one thing on the list. She asked me a simple, direct question: "What do you need right now in order to get one thing done?" That question stopped me in my tracks because I couldn't remember the last time anybody had asked me what I needed. My Aunt, a savvy and sharp housewife and fellow mom whom I had befriended asked again: "What do you need right now to get to one thing on your list on a regular basis? Be specific."

After this intervention from her, I spent one of my treasured hours reflecting on my self-care list again. I rewrote the list, dedicating a single page to each self-care category. I created three columns on each page; in one column I listed each activity in that category, and in the second column I wrote down obstacles. I identified each shoe and piece of clutter in my mudrooms. I asked what was getting in the way of partaking in each activity, writing down things like time, finances, and skills. Then, in the third column, I strategized ways to remove these barriers, listing things either I could do or someone else might do for me.

Three key things emerged for me during this process: First, I realized that I needed the support of a friend or community to be able to remove many of these obstacles. Second, I understood that there were self-care items where I was, in fact, the only obstacle, since they involved issues like motivation, discipline, and self-esteem, to name a few. For these, by taking a realistic look at myself, I realized that I needed someone to hold me accountable when I would not hold myself accountable. Lastly, I realized that some of the items on my list were too ambitious and unrealistic for where I was, and I gave myself permission to remove those items or to leave my plan open for adjustment over time. My self-care plan was not written in stone. It was a living, breathing document that would change over time, as my life and demands changed. It was a document that depended on the support of an entire community.

Not only that, I soon helped everyone in that community formulate their own self-care plans. In time, we would weave together a mutually beneficial safety net of care and support that ensured we could all obtain what we needed, ask for help without guilt, remove obstacles from our path of self-preservation, and hold one another accountable with love and with kind sight. Ultimately, consistently showing up for ourselves lays the foundation for our life's purpose: showing up for others

Get Real About Self-Care

I need to be honest with you: I feel like a total hypocrite writing about self-care. I just spent the last six months traveling the country for a job alone and I can tell you, all of my healthy routines fell away after day three. In the beginning, I got out my yoga mat, and sat under beautiful trees meditating to the sounds of birds. But very quickly, the trip steamrolled into a mess of blown tires, leaky pipes, bored mind and bread butter for breakfast.

Yep.

All the while, I was editing this beautiful June issue of Litvoice magazine.

I'm coming clean with my lack of self-care because I want you to know that I understand how easy it is to de-prioritize your own care. Even when we know what we need in order to show up as our best selves, the practice and routines of care can be the first things to go when life gets crazy—which is right when we need them most.

Prioritising self-care is essential for our mental and physical well-being. We can do this whilst still looking after Mother Earth and being mindful of our impact on the planet. Here are ten eco-friendly and sustainable ways to show yourself and the planet some love.

Practise Mindful Meditation

Find a quiet room, sit in a comfortable position and focus on your breath for a few minutes. Notice what parts of your body feel tense and try to let go, calming your heart rate and clearing your head.

If you can find time to practise meditation every other day, you will notice positive changes in your life, including reduced stress and improved emotional balance.

Meditation can give you a sense of contentment and peace, and this clarity will give you the opportunity to make more sustainable choices in your daily life.

You don't need any equipment, just yourself. This is a fantastic way to look after yourself without using up any resources and even saving a bit of money!

Eco-Friendly Skincare

Eco-friendly skincare brands celebrate the planet by using certified organic ingredients, prioritising sustainable sourcing. So, when you choose these products, you will reduce your own environmental impact.

These natural and organic ingredients also break down more easily in the environment than synthetic ingredients. This means we don't have to worry about the burden these ingredients will have on ecosystems when washed off.

Certified organic brands also tend to favour minimal or biodegradable packaging and the planet will thank you for less plastic waste piling up in the environment.

Eco-friendly products will be kinder to your skin and make you feel rejuvenated. From body balms and face balms to exfoliants, beard balms and cleansers, there is an eco-friendly option for everything.

Spend Time in Nature

Nature is an incredibly powerful force. By immersing ourselves in it, we can soothe feelings of anxiety and lessen mental fatigue.

We can actively strengthen our connection to nature by going for a hike or a walk, or just sitting in a park for a few minutes. Through this, we will be inspired to make more sustainable choices in other aspects of our lives.

In fact, people with a closer relationship to nature have been shown to possess more pro-environmental behaviours such as recycling items and buying seasonal foods.

So, try to get fresh air every day, go for a walk and appreciate the natural world around you.

Digital Detox

It's easy to get caught up with scrolling on your phone for a few too many hours – it happens to the best of us. But it is a slippery slope and once you start, it can be difficult to stop.

Disconnecting from digital devices can do wonders for restoring mental balance and improving concentration and focus.

Plus, you'll be conserving energy and by using your device less, you'll extend its lifespan and will not have to replace it as often. You can reduce the demand for the production of new products, which is also environmentally beneficial.

So, it's time to try a digital detox, to show yourself and the planet some love.

Gratitude Journaling

Another great self-care practice is gratitude journaling. Spend ten to fifteen minutes writing down your thoughts, feelings and the things you're grateful for in life. This will help you to feel more positive towards the world around you.

By cultivating a sense of contentment with what you have, you will also lessen your need for excessive consumption. This can contribute towards making more eco-friendly or ethical choices in the future.

Just grab a pen and paper and then you're good to go.

DIY Spa Day

Get creative and try to make some soothing products packed full of natural ingredients for your very own DIY spa day.

Commercial spas and beauty salons use a ton of water and energy whilst producing significant waste. By pampering yourself at home, you can reduce this environmental impact without sacrificing self-care.

You can make almost anything, from body scrubs to facemasks, using just oatmeal, honey, yoghurt or any of the ingredients you find in your pantry.

Green Cleaning

A clean home can soothe your mind, and make you feel at peace. Your surroundings certainly affect your state of mind, so it is essential to choose the right cleaning products for you.

Synthetic cleaners from your local store can leave a strong smell, sometimes even leaving you uncomfortable. But plant-based cleaning products made from non-toxic ingredients will smell and feel refreshing.

We love the Greenscents range as it's certified organic and palm oil free. These products are also biodegradable, so they will break down nice and easily when washed back into the environment.

This is a great way to show yourself some care, so give it a go.

Plant Care

Taking care of plants means you can connect with the environment, even in an urban setting. By nurturing a living organism, you will appreciate the beauty of the natural world much more.

Plants also offer numerous physical benefits. They act as natural air purifiers by absorbing carbon dioxide and releasing oxygen during photosynthesis. The improved air quality will create a more enjoyable and sustainable living space, having positive effects on your overall sense of calm.

If you really enjoy this, you can go on to create a garden full of fruits and vegetables. Eating healthy foods that you have grown yourself will give you an even greater sense of fulfilment.

Second-Hand Shopping

Another sustainable self-care practice is shopping second hand. You can give second-hand items a new lease on life, and this will prevent them from ending up in landfills, thus reducing waste.

There will be less of a demand for the production of new items, conserving energy and natural resources. This form of a circular economy fosters a more sustainable approach to consumerism. An added benefit is that many second-hand shops also boast interesting and unique pieces, so you can indulge in self-care and buy yourself something you love without breaking the bank or harming the planet.

Yoga

As an ancient practice that is valued by cultures around the world, yoga is the perfect exercise for reconnecting with yourself and finding a sense of inner peace and calm.

Yoga also requires minimal equipment, so as long as you have a mat or soft surface you can give it a go pretty much anywhere.

By focusing on mindful movement, you will feel a deeper connection to yourself. You can also immerse yourself in nature whilst practising it, combining multiple self-care practices to show yourself even more love and care.

It's time to embrace self-care that is kind to you and the Earth. From mindfulness to buying eco-conscious products, there is a sustainable option for everyone. Give any of them a go and see how sustainable self-care has the power to transform your life.

· 154 ·

"Life is a dance of light and shadow, joy and sorrow, each contrasting element adding depth and richness to the tapestry of our experience."

CHAPTER ELEVEN

Simple Mindfulness Practices for Daily Life

How often have you rushed out the door and into your day without even thinking about how you'd like things to go? Before you know it, something or someone has rubbed you the wrong way, and you've reacted automatically with frustration, impatience, or rage—in other words, you've found yourself acting in a way you never intended.

You don't have to be stuck in these patterns. Pausing to practice mindfulness for just a few minutes at different times during the day can help your days be better, more in line with how you'd like them to be.

Explore these five daily practices for bringing more mindfulness into your life:

1) Mindful Wakeup: Start with a Purpose

Intention refers to the underlying motivation for everything we think, say, or do. From the brain's perspective, when we act in unintended ways, there's a disconnect between the faster, unconscious impulses of the lower brain centers and the slower, conscious, wiser abilities of the higher centers like the pre-frontal cortex.

Given that the unconscious brain is in charge of most of our decision-making and behaviors, this practice can help you align your conscious thinking with a primal emotional drive that the lower centers care about. Beyond safety, these include motivations like reward, connection, purpose, self-identity and core values.

Setting an intention—keeping those primal motivations in mind—helps strengthen this connection between the lower and higher centers. Doing so can change your day, making it more likely that your words, actions and responses— especially during moments of difficulty—will be more mindful and compassionate.

This practice is best done first thing in the morning, before checking phones or email.

1. On waking, sit in your bed or a chair in a relaxed posture. Close your eyes and connect with the sensations of your seated body. Make sure your spine is straight, but not rigid.

2. Take three long, deep, nourishing breaths—breathing in through your nose and out through your mouth. Then let your breath settle into its own rhythm, as you simply follow it in and out, noticing the rise and fall of your chest and belly as you breathe.

3. Ask yourself: "What is my intention for today?" Use these prompts to help answer that question, as you think about the people and activities you will face. Ask yourself:

How might I show up today to have the best impact?

What quality of mind do I want to strengthen and develop?

What do I need to take better care of myself?

During difficult moments, how might I be more compassionate to others and myself?

How might I feel more connected and fulfilled?

4. Set your intention for the day. For example, "Today, I will be kind to myself; be patient with others; give

generously; stay grounded; persevere; have fun; eat well," or anything else you feel is important.

5. Throughout the day, check in with yourself. Pause, take a breath, and revisit your intention. Notice, as you become more and more conscious of your intentions for each day, how the quality of your communications, relationships, and mood shifts.

2) Mindful Eating: Enjoy Every Mouthful

It's easy enough to reduce eating to a sensation of bite, chew, and swallow. Who hasn't eaten a plateful of food without noticing what they're doing? Yet eating is one of the most pleasurable experiences we engage in as human beings, and doing it mindfully can turn eating into a far richer experience, satisfying not just the need for nutrition, but more subtle senses and needs. When we bring our full attention to our bodies and what we are truly hungry for, we can nourish all our hungers. Try this:

1. Breathe before eating. We often move from one task right to the other without pausing or taking a breath. By pausing, we slow down and allow for a more calm transition to our meals. Bring your attention inward by closing your eyes, and begin to breathe slowly in and out of your belly for eight to 10 deep breaths before you start your meal.

2. Listen to your body. After breathing, bring your awareness to the physical sensations in your belly. On a scale of 1 to 10, 1 being that you don't feel any physical sensation of hunger and 10 being that you feel very hungry, ask yourself "How hungry am I?" What physical sensations tell you that you are hungry or not hungry (emptiness in stomach, shakiness, no desire to eat, stomach growling, etc.)? Try not to think about when you last ate or what time it is, and really listen to your body, not your thoughts.

3. Eat according to your hunger. Now that you are more in touch with how hungry you are, you can more mindfully choose what to eat, when to eat, and how much to eat. This simple practice can help you tune in to your real needs.

4. Practice peaceful eating. At your next meal, slow down and continue to breathe deeply as you eat. It's not easy to digest or savor your food if you aren't relaxed.

5. If you don't love it, don't eat it. Take your first three bites mindfully, experience the taste, flavors, textures, and how much enjoyment you are receiving from a certain food. Make a mindful choice about what to eat based on what you really enjoy.

3) Mindful Pause: Rewire Your Brain

It's estimated that 95% of our behavior runs on autopilot—something I call "fast brain." That's because neural networks underlie all of our habits, reducing our millions of sensory inputs per second into manageable shortcuts so we can function in this crazy world. These default brain signals are like signaling superhighways, so efficient that they often cause us to relapse into old behaviors before we remember what we meant to do instead.

Mindfulness is the exact opposite of these processes; it's slow brain. It's executive control rather than autopilot, and enables intentional actions, willpower, and decisions. But that takes some practice. The more we activate the slow brain, the stronger it gets. Every time we do something deliberate and new, we stimulate neuroplasticity, activating our grey matter, which is full of newly sprouted neurons that have not yet been groomed for the fast brain.

But here's the problem. While my slow brain knows what is best for me, my fast brain is causing me to shortcut my way through life. So how can we trigger ourselves to be mindful when we need it most? This is where the notion of "behavior design" comes in. It's a way to put your slow brain in the driver's seat. There are two ways to do that—first, slowing down the fast brain by putting obstacles in its way, and second, removing obstacles in the path of the slow brain, so it can gain control.

Shifting the balance to give your slow brain more power takes some work, though. Here are some ways to get started.

1. Trip over what you want to do. If you intend to do some yoga or to meditate, put your yoga mat or your meditation cushion in the middle of your floor so you can't miss it as you walk by.

2. Refresh your triggers regularly. Say you decide to use sticky notes to remind yourself of a new intention. That might work for about a week, but then your fast brain and old habits take over again. Try writing new notes to yourself; add variety or make them funny so they stick with you longer.

3. Create new patterns. You could try a series of "If this, then that" messages to create easy reminders to shift into slow brain. For instance, you might come up with, "If office door, then deep breath," as a way to shift into mindfulness as you are about to start your workday. Or, "If phone rings, take a breath before answering." Each intentional action to shift into mindfulness will strengthen your slow brain.

4) Mindful Workout: Activate Your Mind and Your Muscles

Riding a bike, lifting weights, sweating it out on a treadmill—what do such exercises have in common? For one thing, each can be a mindfulness practice. Whatever the physical activity—dancing the Tango, taking a swim—instead of simply working out to burn calories, master a skill, or improve condition, you can move and breathe in a way that not only gets your blood pumping and invigorates every cell in your body, but also shifts you from feeling busy and distracted to feeling strong and capable.

Ready? The following steps, good for any activity, will help you synchronize body, mind, and nervous system. As you do, you will strengthen your capacity to bring all of your energy to the task at hand.

1. Be clear about your aim. As you tie your laces or pull on your gardening gloves, bring purpose to your activity by consciously envisioning how you want your guide your session. As you climb on your bike you might say, "I am going to breathe deeply and notice the sensation of the breeze and the sun and the passing scenery." As you enter the pool, you might say, "I'm going to pay attention to each stroke, and the sound and feel of the water surrounding me."

2. Warm up (5 minutes). Try any simple moves— jumping jacks, stretching— and concentrate on matching the rhythm of your breath to your movement. By moving rhythmically, your brain activity, heart rate, and nervous system begin to align and stabilize.

3. Settle into a rhythm (10 to 15 minutes). Pick up the intensity, but continue to coordinate your breath and movement. If you have trouble doing this, then simply focus on your breathing for a few minutes. Eventually you'll find your groove.

4. Challenge yourself (10 to 15 minutes). Try faster speed, more repetitions, or heavier weights, depending on what you are doing. Notice how alert and alive you feel when pushing yourself.

5. Cool down (5 minutes). Steadily slow down your pace until you come to a standstill. Notice the way your body

feels. Drink in your surroundings.

6. Rest (5 minutes). Quietly recognize the symphony of sensations flowing in and around you. Practice naming what you feel and sense. Chances are you'll feel awake and alive from head to toe.

5) Mindful Driving: Drive Yourself Calm, Not Crazy

There's nothing like heavy traffic and impatient drivers to trigger the "fight or flight" response. That's why road rage erupts and stress levels soar, while reason is overrun. The worse the traffic, the worse the stress. Los Angeles, where I live, has some of the worst traffic around, and some of the most unserene drivers. Emotions run high, tempers flare, tires squeal.

But it doesn't have to be like that. In fact, the snarliest traffic jam can provide an excellent opportunity to build your mindfulness muscle, increase your sense of connection to others, and restore some balance and perspective.

Here are the steps to a simple behind-the-wheel practice I've been doing for a while. I've found it can work wonders.

1. First, take a deep breath. This simple, yet profound advice helps bring more oxygen into your body and widens the space between the stimulus of the traffic and your heightened stress reaction. In this space lies perspective and choice.

2. Ask yourself what you need. It may be in that moment that you need to feel safe, at ease or you just need some relief. Understanding what you need will bring balance.

3. Give yourself what you need. If ease is what you need, you can scan your body for any tension (not a bad thing to do while driving in any case) and soften any tension or adjust your body as needed. You can sprinkle in some phrases of self-compassion, such as, "May I be at ease, may

I feel safe, may I be happy."

4. Look around and recognize that all the other drivers are just like you. Everyone on the road wants the same thing you do—to feel safe, have a sense of ease, and to be happy. Chances are you'll see a number of fellow drivers who look a bit agitated, but you might also catch that one who is singing or actually smiling, and this will dissipate some of your own stress immediately. You can apply to all of them what you just offered to yourself, saying, "May you be at ease, may you feel safe, may you be happy."

5. Take another deep breath. In 15 seconds or less, you can turn around your mood by applying these simple tips. When you feel the frustration of traffic rising, choose whatever you need to work on, and offer that condition to others. If you need to feel safe, say, "May I be safe, may you be safe, may we all be safe." Breathe in, breathe out, you've sowed a seed of happiness.

"In the silence of meditation, we commune
with the essence of existence, tapping into
the boundless reservoir of peace, wisdom,
and love that lies within."

Cultivating Habits for a Happy Mind

Happiness is not merely a fleeting emotion; it is a state of being that can be cultivated through intentional habits and practices. Cultivating habits for a happy mind involves adopting behaviors and mindsets that promote positive emotions, resilience, and overall well-being. In this essay, we will explore various habits and practices that can contribute to a happy mind. By incorporating these habits into daily life, individuals can nurture their happiness and experience lasting joy and fulfillment.

Gratitude Practice:

Gratitude is a powerful habit that can shift our focus from what is lacking to what is present in our lives. Practicing gratitude involves intentionally acknowledging and appreciating the positive aspects and blessings, both big and small. Keeping a gratitude journal, expressing gratitude to others, or simply reflecting on things to be grateful for each day can foster a sense of contentment and happiness.

Mindfulness and Meditation:

Mindfulness and meditation are practices that cultivate present-moment awareness and a non-judgmental attitude.

By focusing on the here and now, we can reduce stress, enhance self-awareness, and appreciate the simple joys of life. Regular mindfulness exercises and meditation help calm the mind, improve concentration, and promote overall well-being.

Engaging in Physical Activity:

Regular physical activity is not only essential for physical health but also has profound effects on mental well-being. Exercise releases endorphins, the brain's natural feel-good chemicals, which can elevate mood and reduce stress and anxiety. Engaging in activities that you enjoy, whether it's walking, dancing, or playing a sport, can boost happiness and contribute to a healthy mind.

Nurturing Positive Relationships:

Positive relationships play a crucial role in our happiness and well-being. Cultivating healthy and supportive connections with family, friends, and community members fosters a sense of belonging, love, and support. Actively investing time and effort into nurturing these relationships through regular communication, acts of kindness, and quality time together can contribute to a happy mind.

Engaging in Acts of Kindness:

Engaging in acts of kindness not only benefits others but also promotes happiness within ourselves. Acts of kindness can be as simple as offering a helping hand, listening attentively to someone, or volunteering for a charitable cause. These acts create a positive ripple effect, fostering a sense of purpose, compassion, and joy.

Practicing Self-Care:

Self-care is a fundamental habit for maintaining a happy mind. It involves prioritizing our physical, emotional, and mental well-being. Engaging in activities that recharge and rejuvenate us, such as taking baths, practicing hobbies, getting enough sleep, and setting healthy boundaries, helps prevent burnout and promotes a sense of self-worth and happiness.

Continuous Learning and Personal Growth:

Engaging in continuous learning and personal growth nurtures a happy mind by providing opportunities for intellectual stimulation, skill development, and personal fulfillment. Pursuing interests, acquiring new knowledge, and setting meaningful goals not only boost confidence but also cultivate a sense of purpose and accomplishment.

Cultivating Optimism and Positive Thinking:

Our mindset and thought patterns significantly impact our happiness. Cultivating optimism and positive thinking involves consciously choosing to focus on the positive aspects of situations, reframing challenges as opportunities for growth, and practicing positive self-talk. By nurturing a positive mindset, we can approach life with resilience, hope, and a happier outlook.

In today's digital age, excessive screen time and constant connectivity can negatively impact our mental well-being. Taking intentional breaks from technology, such as implementing digital detoxes, setting boundaries for screen usage, and allocating time for unplugged activities, allows for relaxation, mindfulness, and deeper connections with oneself and others.

Seeking Help and Support:

Recognizing when to seek help and support is crucial for maintaining a happy mind. It's okay to reach out to trusted friends, family, or mental health professionals when needed. Seeking therapy, counseling, or joining support groups can provide valuable guidance, insights, and tools for managing challenges and enhancing overall well-being.

Cultivating habits for a happy mind is an ongoing journey that requires conscious effort and dedication. By incorporating gratitude, mindfulness, physical activity, nurturing relationships, acts of kindness, self-care, continuous learning, positive thinking, technology moderation, and seeking support, individuals can foster happiness, resilience, and overall well-being. Remember, cultivating these habits takes time and consistency, but the rewards of a happy mind are immeasurable. Embrace the power of these habits and let them guide you towards a life of lasting joy, fulfillment, and happiness.

Do you, like many people, have a mental list of things you think you need in order to be truly happy? There are many externals our society teaches us to chase: success, wealth, fame, power, good looks, romantic love. But are they really the keys to happiness?

The research says no, at least when it comes to long-term happiness. A prestigious award, a big raise, an exciting new relationship, a fancy new car, losing weight, these things can make us feel great at first, but the thrill doesn't last very long. Human beings are quick to adapt to new circumstances—a quality that has helped us survive and thrive. But it also means that the positive things that initially make us happier soon become our new normal and we return to our old happiness baseline.

However, researchers in the field of positive psychology have found that you can genuinely increase your happiness and overall satisfaction with life—and it doesn't require a winning lottery ticket or some other drastic change of circumstances. What it takes is an inner change of perspective and attitude. And that's truly good news, because it's something anyone can do.

Myths and facts about happiness

There are a lot of myths out there about what will make you happy. So, before we embark on a tour of the strategies that do work for boosting happiness, let's dispense with the things that don't.

Myth:

Money will make you happy.

Fact:

It's stressful when you're worried about money. In order to be happy, you do need enough of it to cover your basic needs: things like food, shelter, and clothing. But once you have enough money to be comfortable, getting more money isn't going to make much of a difference in how happy you are. For example, studies of lottery winners show that after a relatively short period of time, they are no happier than they were before their win.

Myth:

You need a relationship in order to be happy.

Fact:

Being in a healthy, supportive love relationship does contribute to happiness, but it's not true that you can't be happy and fulfilled if you're single. Indeed, singles who have meaningful friendships and pursuits are happier than people in mismatched romantic relationships. It's also important to note that even a good marriage or romantic partnership doesn't lead to a permanent, intense happiness boost. Expecting your partner to deliver your happily-ever-after may actually harm the relationship in the long-run. You—not your partner or your family members—are responsible for your own happiness.

Myth:

Happiness declines with age.

Fact:

Contrary to popular belief, people tend to get happier with age. Study after study confirms that seniors experience more positive emotions and fewer (and less intense) negative emotions than young people and middle-aged adults. Generally, older adults are also more satisfied with their lives, less sensitive to stress, and more emotionally stable. Even with the losses that come with age, it is the happiest time of life for many people.

Myth:

Some people are just happier than others and there's nothing you can do to change that.

Fact:

Genetics do play a role in happiness. Current research suggests that people are born with a certain happiness "set point." But that only accounts for about half of our happiness level. Another 10% is due to life circumstances. That leaves 40% that is determined by your actions and choices. That's a lot of control!

Tip 1: Train your brain to be more positive

Our brains are wired to notice and remember the things that are wrong. It's a survival mechanism that helped keep our cave-dwelling ancestors safe in a world where there were many physical threats. But in today's comparatively safe world, this biological predisposition to focus on the negative contributes to stress and unhappiness.

While we can't change our nature, we can train our brains to be more positive. This doesn't mean putting on a smiley face and whistling a happy tune no matter what's going on. You don't have to ignore reality or pretend things are wonderful even when they're not. But just as dwelling on negative things fuels unhappiness (and plays a big role in depression and anxiety), choosing to notice, appreciate, and anticipate goodness is a powerful happiness booster.

Speak to a Licensed Therapist

BetterHelp is an online therapy service that matches you to licensed, accredited therapists who can help with depression, anxiety, relationships, and more. Take the assessment and get matched with a therapist in as little as 48 hours.

Express gratitude

Teaching yourself to become more grateful can make a huge difference in your overall happiness. The research shows that gratitude helps you experience more positive emotions, decrease depression, feel better about yourself, improve your relationships, and strengthen your immune system. A recent study revealed that gratitude even makes you smarter about how you spend your money.

There are a number of simple exercises you can practice to increase and cultivate an attitude of gratitude.

Give sincere thanks to others. When someone goes above and beyond or does something to make your day easier, be quick to verbalize your thanks and appreciation. Not only will it make the person feel good, it will give you a happiness lift, too. It's an instant reward to see how expressing gratitude makes a positive difference in someone else's day. It makes you realize that we're all connected and that what you do matters.

Keep a gratitude journal. It may sound cheesy, but writing down the good things that happened to you during the day really works. Research shows that keeping a gratitude journal is a powerful technique that instantly makes you feel happier, more connected to others, and genuinely appreciative.

Count your blessings. Make it a habit to regularly reflect on the things you have to be thankful for. Bring to mind all the good people, experiences, and things in your life, both now and in the past. Focus on the blessings both big and small, from the people who love you, to the roof over your head and the food on your table. You will soon see it's a pretty long list.

Write a letter of gratitude. Think of someone who did something that changed your life for the better who you never properly thanked. Write a thoughtful letter of gratitude expressing what the person did, how it affected you, and what it still means to you. Then deliver the letter. Positive psychology expert Martin Seligman recommends reading the letter in person for the most dramatic increase in happiness.

Find the positive in a negative event from your past. Even the most painful circumstances can teach us positive lessons. Reevaluate a negative event from your past with an eye for what you learned or how you became stronger, wiser, or more compassionate. When you can find meaning in even the bad things you've experienced, you will be happier and more grateful.

Tip 2: Nurture and enjoy your relationships

Relationships are one of the biggest sources of happiness in our lives. Studies that look at happy people bear this out. The happier the person, the more likely that he or she has a large, supportive circle of family and friends, a fulfilling marriage, and a thriving social life.

That's why nurturing your relationships is one of the best emotional investments you can make. If you make an effort to cultivate and build your connections with others, you will soon reap the rewards of more positive emotions. And as you become happier, you will attract more people and higher-quality relationships, leading to even greater positivity and enjoyment. It's the happiness gift that keeps on giving.

Make a conscious effort to stay connected. In our busy society, it's easy to get caught up in our responsibilities and neglect our relationships. But losing touch with friends is one of the most common end-of-life regrets. Don't let it happen to you. Make an effort to stay connected to the people who make your life brighter. Take the time to call, write, or see each other in person. You'll be happier for it.

Invest in quality time with the people you care about. It's not just the time spent with friends and family that matters; it's how you spend it. Mindlessly vegging out together in front of the TV isn't going to make you closer. People who are in happy relationships talk a lot. They share what's going on in their lives and how they feel. Follow their example and carve out time to talk and enjoy each other's company.

Offer sincere compliments. Think of the things you admire and appreciate about the other person and then tell them. This will not only make the other person happier, it will encourage him or her to be an even better friend or partner. As a practice of gratitude, it will also make you value the relationship more and feel happier.

Seek out happy people. Research shows that happiness is contagious. You can literally catch a good mood (you can also catch a bad mood, but thankfully, sadness is less contagious than happiness). So, make an effort to seek out and spend time with happy people. Before you know it, you'll be feeling the happiness, too.

Take delight in the good fortune of others. One of the things that truly separate healthy, fulfilling relationships from the rest are how the partners respond to each other's good fortune and success. Do you show genuine enthusiasm and interest when your friend or family member experiences something good? Or do you ignore, criticize, or downplay the achievement, feel envious or threatened, or say a quick, "That's great," and then move on? If you'd like closer relationships, pay attention when the other person is excited. Ask questions, relive the experience with the other person, and express your excitement for him or her. Remember, happiness is contagious, so as you share the experience, their joy will become yours.

Tip 3: Live in the moment and savor life's pleasures

Think about a time when you were depressed or anxious. Chances are, you were either dwelling on something negative from the past or worrying about something in the future. In contrast, when you focus on the present moment, you are much more likely to feel centered, happy, and at peace. You're also much more likely to notice the good things that are happening, rather than letting them pass by unappreciated or unobserved. So how do you start to live more in the moment and savor the good things life has to offer?

Meditate

Mindfulness meditation is a powerful technique for learning to live in and enjoy the moment. And you don't have to be religious or even spiritual to reap its benefits. No pan flutes, chanting, or yoga pants required.

Simply speaking, meditation is exercise for your brain. When practiced regularly, meditation appears to decrease activity in the areas of the brain associated with negative thoughts, anxiety, and depression. At the same time, it increases activity in the areas associated with joy, contentment, and peace. It also strengthens areas of the brain in charge of managing emotions and controlling attention.

What's more, being mindful makes you more fully engaged in the here-and-now and more aware and appreciative of good things.

Here are a few mindfulness exercises that can help you get started:

Body scan – Body scanning cultivates mindfulness by focusing your attention on various parts of your body. Like progressive muscle relaxation, you start with your feet and work your way up. However, instead of tensing and relaxing your muscles, you simply focus on the way each part of your body feels without labeling the sensations as either "good" or "bad".

Walking meditation – You don't have to be seated or still to meditate. In walking meditation, mindfulness involves being focused on the physicality of each step — the sensation of your feet touching the ground, the rhythm of your breath while moving, and the feeling of the wind against your face.

Mindful eating – If you reach for food when you're under stress or gulp your meals down in a rush, try eating mindfully. Sit down at the table and focus your full attention on the meal (no TV, newspapers, or eating on the run). Eat slowly, taking the time to fully enjoy and concentrate on each bite.

Notice and savor small pleasures

If you adopt a mindfulness meditation practice, you will automatically begin to notice and savor life's pleasures more. But there are other things you can do to increase your awareness and enjoyment.

Adopt enjoyable daily rituals. Build moments of enjoyment into your day with pleasurable rituals. These can be very simple things like lingering over a cup of coffee in the morning, taking a short stroll in the sunshine during your lunch hour, or playing with your dog when you get home. It doesn't matter what you do, as long as you enjoy and appreciate it.

Minimize multi-tasking. Savoring requires your full attention, which is impossible when you're trying to do multiple things. For example, if you're eating a delicious meal while distractedly surfing the Internet, you're not going to get as much pleasure out of the food as you could have. Focus on one thing at a time in order to truly maximize your enjoyment.

Stop to smell the roses. It may be an old cliché, but it's good advice. You'll appreciate good things more if you stop whatever you're doing for a moment to appreciate and luxuriate in them. It will enhance your pleasure, even if you can only spare a few seconds. And if you can share the moment with others, that's even better. Shared pleasure is powerful.

Replay happy memories. You don't have to limit your savoring to things that are happening now. Remembering and reminiscing about happy memories and experiences from your past leads to more positive emotions in the present.

Tip 4: Focus on helping others and living with meaning

There is something truly fulfilling in helping others and feeling like your actions are making a difference for the better in the world. That's why people who assist those in need and give back to others and their communities tend to be happier. In addition, they also tend to have higher self-esteem and general psychological well-being.

Here are some ways to live a more altruistic, meaningful life:

Volunteer. Happiness is just one of the many benefits of volunteering. You'll get the most out of the experience by volunteering for an organization that you believe in and that allows you to contribute in a meaningful way.

Practice kindness. Look for ways to be more kind, compassionate, and giving in your daily life. This can be something as small as brightening a stranger's day with a smile or going out of your way to do a favor for a friend.

Listen to HelpGuide's loving kindness meditation.

Play to your strengths. The happiest people know what their unique strengths are and build their lives around activities that allow them to use those strengths for the greater good. There are many different kinds of strengths, including kindness, curiosity, honesty, creativity, love of learning, perseverance, loyalty, optimism, and humor.

Go for the flow. Research shows that flow, a state of complete immersion and engagement in an activity, is closely associated with happiness. Flow happens when you're actively engaged in something that is intrinsically rewarding and challenging yet still attainable. Anything that completely captivates you and engages your full attention can be a flow activity.

Tip 5: Take better care of your health

You can be happy even when you're suffering from illness or bad health, but that doesn't mean you should ignore the aspects of your health that are in your control. Exercise and sleep are particularly important when it comes to happiness.

Make exercise a regular habit

Exercise isn't just good for the body. It also has a powerful effect on mental well-being. People who exercise regularly are happier across the board. Plus, they're also less stressed, angry, anxious, and depressed.

[Read: Best Exercises for Health and Weight Loss]

It doesn't really matter what kind of exercise you do, so long as you do it regularly. For best results, aim for an hour of exercise at least five days a week. If you find something you enjoy, you'll be more likely to stick to it. So don't think you're limited to going to the gym or lacing up jogging shoes. Find something that suits your lifestyle and preferences. It could be taking a dance class, shooting hoops, walking in nature, joining a community sports league, playing tennis, running with your dog, swimming laps at the pool, hiking, biking, or doing yoga in the park. If you're having trouble thinking of activities you enjoy, think back to when you were a kid. What sports or games did you like to play?

Get the sleep you need

Getting quality sleep every night directly affects your happiness, vitality, and emotional stability during the day. When you're sleep deprived, you're much more susceptible to stress. It's harder to be productive, think creatively, and make wise decisions. How much sleep do you need? According to sleep scientists, the average person needs at least 7.5 – 9 hours each night.

"In the theater of the mind, we are both the actors and the audience, playing out our roles on the stage of consciousness, while observing the drama of life with curiosity and wonder."

Thanks To Readers

Dear Readers,

As I reflect on the journey of writing "Theory of a Happy Mind," I am overwhelmed with gratitude for each and every one of you who has taken the time to read these pages. This book is the culmination of countless hours of introspection, research, and personal growth, and to have it resonate with you means more to me than words can express.

At its core, "Theory of a Happy Mind" is a manifesto for living a life filled with purpose, positivity, and fulfillment. It's a roadmap for navigating the complexities of the human experience and finding joy in the present moment. But more than that, it's a testament to the power of the mind and the limitless potential we all possess to create our own happiness.

Writing this book was not without its challenges. There were moments of self-doubt, periods of writer's block, and days when the words just wouldn't flow. But through it all, I remained steadfast in my belief in the importance of spreading positivity and sharing the insights I've gained on my own journey to happiness.

I want to extend my deepest gratitude to each of you who has joined me on this journey. Whether you picked up this book seeking guidance, inspiration, or simply a moment of solace, I am honored to have been a part of your life in this way. Your support and encouragement have been the driving force behind every word written, and for that, I am truly thankful.

To those who have shared their own stories of struggle and triumph, thank you for your vulnerability and your courage. Your willingness to open your hearts and minds has created a community of support and understanding that is truly remarkable. Together, we have shown that no matter what challenges we may face, we are never alone in our quest for happiness.

I also want to express my gratitude to my family and friends, whose unwavering love and support have sustained me throughout this journey. Your belief in me has been a constant source of strength and inspiration, and I am forever grateful for the countless ways you have lifted me up and cheered me on.

Finally, I want to thank each and every one of you for your willingness to embrace the message of this book and to take steps toward living a happier, more fulfilling life. Remember that happiness is not a destination to be reached, but a journey to be enjoyed. It is found in the simple moments of everyday life, in the connections we forge with others, and in the gratitude we cultivate for all that we have.

As you close the pages of "Theory of a Happy Mind," I hope you carry with you the lessons learned and the wisdom gained. May you continue to nurture your own happiness, cultivate positivity in all that you do, and spread joy to those around you. Together, we can create a world filled with happiness, one mind at a time.

With love and gratitude,
Agrata Shukla

"As I close this book, I wish to share that its soul was born in the hills of Uttarakhand — a place where I've lived some of the best years of my life. Every brushstroke of my art, every thought behind these words, carries the whisper of its winds, the song of its trees, and the stillness of its cold embrace. That land is not just inspiration — it is home. If I ever have to choose where to rest forever, it will be there."
- With love and gratitude,
Agrata Shukla